LEAN SIX SIGMA BEGINNER'S GUIDE

A Beginner's Guide to Understanding And Practicing Lean Six Sigma

Jim Hall & Tina Scott

Table of Contents

Introduction

For the majority of people who are involved in business, "Lean" and "Six Sigma" are not new terms. Some may have heard about these concepts but don't really understand what they are all about. In certain cases, people and organizations try to haphazardly implement one or the other to solve their problems, and unfortunately, rarely achieve the results they want.

If your organization is considering starting a Lean Six Sigma initiative, then this is the book for you. This book is written with the purpose of introducing you to Lean Six Sigma. You will discover how different industries can adopt strategies and techniques to improve production, service delivery, and growth, all in the name of satisfying customer needs and achieving the company's goals.

Before you dive deeper into this book, you will need to understand the foundational concepts of Lean Six Sigma. Simply put, Lean is a methodology that emphasizes manufacturing a product or implementing a process faster and with greater efficiency. Six Sigma, on the other hand, is a method of improving the quality of a business process. These two disciplines are combined to create a business method that improves the quality of your processes while turbo-charging your company's growth and profitability.

This book explores the foundations of Lean Six Sigma in a manner that is easy to understand for beginners. Most books written for beginners tend to make assumptions as to the level of knowledge the reader has regarding the subject matter. We have decided to assume that the reader has heard about Lean Six Sigma but doesn't really understand the tools and techniques of the methodology. For this reason, the book explores in some detail the concepts of Lean thinking and Six Sigma methodology in the first few chapters. The intention is to prepare the reader adequately before the book dives into the nitty-gritty aspects of Lean Six Sigma. This book breaks down the basic components of Lean Six Sigma such that people who have never studied Lean or Six Sigma will grasp the concepts with relative ease. If you have some knowledge about Lean Six Sigma, you will still find this book extremely useful.

The book is split into four parts. It starts off with the basics, the language you have to get used to, and the elements that define Lean Six Sigma. Once the basics have been covered, the book goes deeper into the principles, tools, and techniques that every organization should implement to achieve fast and long-term results. Beginners should start from the beginning and work their way through, but if you are somewhat familiar with the basics, you can start with whatever parts you want.

The world is changing rapidly and more so the business world. Any company that wants to survive these shark-infested waters we live in today must step up and put its house in order. Customers no longer tolerate low-quality products and services. It is an expectation that a company must provide high quality with fast delivery at a minimal cost. If you have been looking for a competitive edge, then Lean Six Sigma is the answer.

Apply the concepts you learn here to create a more effective synergy between Lean and Six Sigma. If you can put these methods into practice in your day-to-day operations, you will be able to exploit whatever opportunities there are to improve your business processes.

Part I: The Foundations of Lean Six Sigma

Chapter 1: What is Lean Six Sigma?

If you have been in business for a while now, you most likely have come across the term Six Sigma. It is a quality improvement method that is commonly used today. Lean is well known in manufacturing circles and is primarily focused on the speed and efficiency of the process. To those who have never come across these funny-sounding terms, rest assured that by the end of Part I of this book, you will have a firm grasp of what Lean Six Sigma is all about.

Lean Six Sigma is a combination of both the Lean and Six Sigma philosophies. This creates a powerful improvement concept that applies data-driven tools to solve problems, transform processes, and reduce costs. The most critical aspect, of course, is finding the perfect combination of both Lean and Six Sigma.

Most people view Lean Six Sigma as an improvement method that is dependent on data to find and eliminate problems in a business process. It can also be described as an improvement engine that creates an entirely fresh set of functions and systems within an organization in order to generate results. Lean Six Sigma helps a company achieve its goals and at the same time meet customer needs.

Lean Six Sigma can be defined as a precise and controlled approach that is geared toward enabling managers and team leaders improve quality and performance and also solve complex challenges. It enables the organization to apply the right tools in the right way in order to improve a business process. Instead of seeing Lean Six Sigma as a one-off tool or technique that brings immediate results, consider it as a set of principles and concepts that need to be implemented every day to achieve organizational goals.

The Lean Six Sigma approach requires a fundamental shift in the attitude and thinking of an organization's employees, starting from the top hierarchy all the way down to the bottom. Once the thinking has changed, then the way people do things will change and the end result will be a dramatic turnaround in results. The only constant will be the organization's goals, which essentially should be creating value for the customer and improving the efficiency and effectiveness of the business.

The Case for Lean Six Sigma

There are a number of questions that most people usually ask when applying the Lean Six Sigma approach in an organization, for example:

- "Why should an organization adopt Lean Six Sigma as a way of doing business?"

- "Why not just pick one of the two philosophies instead of both?"

- "Can the two philosophies even work together?"

Lean Six Sigma has the potential to help any organization grow its revenue, reduce costs, enhance customer satisfaction, improve delivery time, and develop better decision-making skills. This is just a tip of the iceberg when it comes to the upside of using Lean Six Sigma. All over the world, organizations in diverse sectors of the economy are applying Lean Six Sigma strategies.

While some quarters think that either Lean or Six Sigma on its own is enough, the evidence to the contrary is overwhelming. Lean is a great philosophy, and so is Six Sigma, but the truth is that times have changed. In today's business climate, what worked great yesterday is not guaranteed to work tomorrow. Combining the two approaches creates a win-win situation since each brings something different to the table.

Lean provides a strategy that helps the organization create an environment where waste is eliminated and business processes improved. Employees are motivated to continuously learn so that they can identify opportunities for adding value to the organizational system. Six Sigma, on the other hand, provides a scientific method to help quantify problems, make fact-based decisions, minimize variation, and discover the root causes and solutions of variations. It enables the organization to focus its efforts on the areas that have the greatest potential for improvement.

There is genuine synergy between Lean and Six Sigma. They both focus on satisfying the customer's needs and improving the processes within the organization. They also share similar quality improvement steps. Though there are a few differences between them, the points of commonality greatly overshadow these variations. What every organization must remember is that Lean and Six Sigma need each other, because where one is weak, the other is strong.

The next two chapters discuss both these approaches in greater detail so that your understanding of each is sharpened. This will be extremely useful when we start looking into the intricate elements, tools, and strategies that define Lean Six Sigma.

Chapter 2: Understanding Lean Thinking

The Lean philosophy is a group of business methods, strategies, and practices that are primarily focused on continuous improvement and eliminating waste within a company. Despite popular belief that the Lean model is the preserve of the manufacturing and production industry, it is a concept that can be adapted to suit any type of business. Lean encompasses the various aspects of operations, such as internal functions, supply networks, and consumer value chains.

Due to its origins, the Lean philosophy tends to make a lot of references to manufacturing situations. In reality, however, the Lean approach is one that every type of business organization can find useful due to its vigilant and rigorous methods of reducing waste and improving efficiency. Lean is now used in almost every industry, including construction, healthcare, aerospace, retail, banking, and government.

In order to appreciate fully the Lean philosophy, it is important to look back at its origins. This management philosophy came out from the Toyota Production System (TPS), which had a very successful automobile manufacturing and operations system. The core aspect of the Lean philosophy was to try to reduce three types of variation in manufacturing: *muda*, *mura*, and *muri*.

Muda is a Japanese word that means uselessness or futility. In business, this would represent waste. In order to reduce and eliminate waste, it is necessary to first clearly separate activities that are considered value-adding from those that have been identified as being wasteful.

Mura refers to unevenness in business workflow processes. This form of waste can cause needless downtimes or phases of unnecessary strain on employees, processes, and equipment. From a managerial perspective, unevenness leads to one of the biggest challenges for businesses – uncertainty. It is difficult to plan ahead and run a successful business if the levels of uncertainty are too high. Any kind of interruption in the workflow process can easily lead to a reduction in the ability of an organization to respond to customer needs. If a customer orders a product and the expectation is that delivery will be made by a set date, throwing uncertainty into the mix suddenly causes chaos and delays. For a manufacturing organization to overcome *mura*, it must seriously consider the layout of its facilities and assembly protocol. For any other kind of business, there has to be a methodology for understanding processes better and improving the ability to foresee potential problems.

Muri refers to waste resulting from overburdening a system or through lack of understanding its capabilities. If a production system or business process becomes overworked, it is inevitable that wear and tear will occur, both on the machines as well as personnel. An extremely high workload can result in system failure and production of a high number of defective products. When *mura* and *muri* combine, bottlenecks crop up all over the organization. The best way to avoid straining the machines or employees is to make sure that the focus remains on only those activities that add value. The organization must also minimize waste in other relevant areas.

Another Lean concept that goes hand-in-hand with waste identification and reduction is *Kaizen*. Kaizen refers to continuous improvement. It involves creating a culture where an individual or organization chooses to improve themselves on a consistent basis. This is a concept that has been adopted by almost every industry, from global multinational businesses to personal trainers.

The Lean philosophy incorporates numerous tools, but the major factor affecting its impact in an organization is an attentive mindset. Everyone in the organization, from CEO to shop steward, must be vigilant when it comes to eliminating waste, continuously improving, and effecting positive change.

Lean and the TPS Approach

In order to further comprehend Lean thinking, we must look into the tools and terms used in the Japanese Toyota Production System. The TPS methodology is essentially geared toward understanding how processes work, identifying ways of improving them, and making the processes smoother and faster. If there are any activities in the process that are unnecessary, then they have to be eliminated.

On the other hand, every business that adopts the TPS approach must realize that it is not a panacea for all the problems within the organization. It is not about the elements on their own, but how they are all brought together to create a system that is consistently put into practice daily. The principles must be embedded into the thinking of everyone within the organization. There must be action and implementation.

Utilizing the Human Potential

People form the core of the TPS approach. In order to achieve excellent organizational results, the employees must be trained on how to adopt values and beliefs that will bring about a strong and stable organizational culture. The company has to make an effort to constantly reinforce this new culture so that it becomes a permanent feature on its business landscape.

Every organization must always remember that it is the people who create value. It is people who implement processes and use equipment and technology. To root out waste from within requires establishing the right culture and setting, where employees are innovative, engaged, and perform work that is meaningful.

The Lean philosophy is often mistaken as a set of tools and techniques. However, Lean is first and foremost about people. There are companies that have failed to grasp this simple idea and have suffered the consequences. Lean requires everyone in the organization to change their mindset and then use the tools to eliminate waste and improve customer value. The organization must respect its people, continually educating, training, challenging, and empowering them. Any organization that thinks itself Lean has to see its people as its most prized asset, and this asset must be stimulated, celebrated, and compensated properly.

The Terms You Need To Know

Heijunka

Heijunka means "leveling" in Japanese, and is the foundation of the TPS model. It is designed to help organizations meet customer demand with minimal waste in the production process. Most experts agree that heijunka should be considered during the latter stages of implementing a Lean strategy. It works best after the organization has identified, solidified, and refined their value streams, and the Lean philosophy is already entrenched into the organizational culture. It involves three ideas:

- Leveling – This refers to minimizing variations in the volume of production so as to make planning easier. It is aimed at ensuring that production is a predictable process throughout the month rather than a "peak" and "trough" affair. In other words, a company should produce the same average number of a product every day rather than vary its production numbers.

- Sequencing – This refers to combining the type of work done. The aim is to create a process where production matches consumer demand. Every product is produced according to a particular sequence, and this sequence is a by-product of customer demand. Tasks are processed according to date so that customer demand is met.

- Standardization and Stability – This refers to ensuring that work standards are maintained at a constant level. It involves reducing variation in the standards of processes and continuously employing best practices. Once standardization has been accomplished within an organization, the business processes can then be stabilized, and finally improved.

Jidoka

Jidoka means humanized automation and involves preventing defects in products and stopping work if any are detected. By stopping the work process the moment a problem occurs, the cause of the problem can be identified immediately. The root causes can then be eliminated and the process improved. Jidoka is one of the two pillars of the TPS system and has two major elements:

- Automation – This means automation with human intelligence. The equipment being used in the production process is designed to automatically differentiate between good and defective products. There is no need for a human operator to stand and watch over the machine, thus allowing one person to supervise several machines at once. This form of innovation can be seen with printing machines that automatically stop printing when the ink runs out.

- Stop at every abnormality – If a defect is spotted, an employee can stop the entire production line so that the problem can be resolved immediately. This may seem like an extreme measure, but if the company is batch-processing a product, the potential for massive defects is averted by fixing the root cause as early as possible.

Just-in-Time (JIT)
This is the second pillar of the TPS model. JIT is a management philosophy that involves producing goods for customers at the right time, of the right quality, and in the right quantity. The customer may be the final buyer of the product or simply another link in the production chain. It was originally developed and refined by Taiichi Ohno as a way of meeting customer needs with minimal delays. Nowadays, JIT is used to refer to production with minimal waste. There are three major elements of JIT:

- Single piece flow – Every worker on the processing line checks the quality of the work prior to handing off the product to the next person. In case there is a defect in a product, Jidoka comes into play. The process stops, the defect is corrected, and measures put in place to prevent future problems. This is quite different from the conventional batch processing system where the entire batch is produced and checked for defects when the process is complete. This causes extensive delays in time and errors can only be detected much later. The root cause of the problem may be difficult to identify since the process was not stopped immediately. Single piece flow allows the root cause to be identified early on, thus preventing wastage of an entire batch of defective goods.

- Pull production – This is where a product is produced only when it is needed and in the exact quantity that customers demand. The customer pulls the items required from the supply, thus preventing costly storage of goods that are not immediately needed. Overproduction leads to waste and bottlenecks downstream.

- Takt time – Takt is a German word that refers to an interval of time. It is used to alert people to the urgency of an activity according to customer demand. Takt describes how frequent a good or service needs to be finished so as to meet customer demand.

The 5 Principles of Lean

In order for an organization to implement the Lean philosophy, it has to take into consideration these five principles:

1. Specify the value of a product from the perspective of the end consumer. Value is defined by the customer and not the organization. It is necessary for the organization to understand its processes, improve flow, and prevent waste.

2. Determine every step in the value stream for a particular family of products, and get rid of those steps that are not adding value.

3. Ensure that the steps that add value to the process follow each other in a tight sequence in order for the product to flow smoothly to the customer.

4. Once flow has been established, allow customers to pull value from the processes.

5. Start the process all over again and repeat continuously until perfection is achieved. The aim should be the creation of perfect value without any waste.

Lean thinking provides an organization with effective ways to enhance value for customers by eliminating waste and smoothening out the process flow. In the next chapter, we look at main ideas behind Lean's close cousin, Six Sigma.

Chapter 3: Understanding Six Sigma

Organizations and businesses exist to serve their constituencies. These constituencies may be the owners or shareholders of the company or customers who buy products and services. For this reason, every organization must create value. An effective and efficient organization must ensure that its output is greater than its inputs, and the value added is created using minimal resources.

The role of Six Sigma is to enable management to apply scientific, problem-solving principles to create maximum value at the minimum cost. This technique involves applying a structured methodology to improve any aspect of an existing business process, as well as designing new products and processes of greater quality and performance.

What is Six Sigma?

Six Sigma can be defined as a thorough, focused and extremely effective application of proven quality techniques and methodologies. The aim of Six Sigma is to eliminate every possible defect and error in the performance of a business. Sigma, σ, is a Greek letter that is used as a measure of variability. The performance of a company is measured by the sigma level of its processes. In the past, most companies were quite content to maintain a sigma level of three or four, even though such companies were creating tens of thousands of defective products per million opportunities. Due to increased customer expectation, Six Sigma has set a standard of 3.4 problems per million opportunities.

The tools and techniques that Six Sigma uses are applied within the framework of a performance improvement model referred to as DMAIC.

D – **Define** the goals of the improvement activity.

M – **Measure** the existing system.

A – **Analyze** the system to determine how to eliminate the gap between current system/process performance and the end goal.

I – **Improve** the system.

C – **Control** the new system.

Why Six Sigma?

Back in the 1970s, a Motorola plant that manufactured TV sets was taken over by a Japanese company, which quickly began implementing drastic changes to the way the factory was run. The new Japanese managers managed to get the factory to produce TV sets that had 1/20th as many defects as before. Surprisingly, this great reduction in defects was achieved using the same workers, designs, and technology as before. In fact, costs were reduced during the same period. It became evident that the problem had always been the management of the factory.

The majority of people assume that Six Sigma is just about quality as defined conventionally. Quality has traditionally been defined as "conformance to internal requirements." However, this definition of quality does not give an accurate representation of what Six Sigma really is about.

Six Sigma involves enabling an organization to improve its process efficiency and customer value so that it increases its profits. In order to link this objective with quality, a fresh definition has to be introduced. When applying Six Sigma principles, quality is defined as "the value added by a productive endeavor." There are two types of quality: *potential* and *actual* quality. Potential quality refers to the maximum value that can possibly be added for every unit of input. Actual quality refers to the current value being added to every unit of input. The difference between the two is what is known as *waste*.

The focus of Six Sigma is eliminating waste and improving the quality of products and services within an organization. Unlike the senseless cost-cutting programs that the majority of companies like to engage in, Six Sigma does not reduce the value *and* the quality of products and services. Six Sigma places emphasis on identifying and eliminating those costs that do not add value to customers even as quality is improved. Most organizations are willing to sacrifice quality just to reduce costs, but Six Sigma does not conform to this thinking. It focuses on customer needs, preventing defects, reducing cycle time, and saving on costs.

The sigma level of a company is directly related to its quality level. As described earlier, a Six Sigma company will fail to achieve its requirements about 3 times out of every one million transactions. The average company, which is usually classified as four sigma, fails to meet its requirements about 6,210 times per million transactions. The difference is clearly staggering! Studies have shown that such companies also tend to experience extremely high operating costs, with 25-40% of their revenue being used to fix problems. In stark contrast, Six Sigma companies spend a mere 5% of their revenues on fixing problems. This gap is known as the cost of poor quality, and research has shown that the gap costs four sigma companies about 10 billion dollars every year.

One question that should be asked is this – why is it necessary to relate costs to sigma levels? Simply put, sigma levels are indicators of error rates, and as every business person knows, fixing errors costs money. As the sigma level of a company goes up, its error rates, and by extension, its operating costs drops sharply. The truth is that in today's business environment, nobody will tolerate errors and defects as a normal part of production!

The Philosophy of Six Sigma

To implement Six Sigma, scientific methods must be applied when designing and operating business processes and management systems. This helps employees to provide better value to both the shareholders as well as customers. An example of a scientific method is as described below:

1. A critical aspect of the business or market is identified.

2. A hypothesis consistent with the observations is developed.

3. Predictions are made based on the hypothesis.

4. Experiments are conducted to test the predictions. More observations are made and recorded. Based on the new data collected, the hypothesis is modified. If there are any variations, use statistical tools to distinguish between signal and noise.

5. Steps 3 and 4 are repeated until no discrepancies exist between hypothesis and actual results.

If such a method can be applied over a period of time, an organization will be able to develop a viable theory that will enable it to understand its customers as well as its business processes. In reality, most organizations make decisions but cannot provide hard data to explain these decisions. However, if a scientific method like the one above is continuously implemented, it creates a fundamental attitude shift that causes management to question whether what they know is the same as what the data shows.

The philosophy of Six Sigma shifts everyone's focus onto the company's stakeholders – the customers and the owners. If the business processes and management systems are designed properly and run by happy employees, the stakeholders will be satisfied. Yet the majority of traditional organizations actually believe that they already do this. The difference is that a Six Sigma organization takes a more systematic and rigorous approach when implementing this philosophy.

Taking Action

The business world moves at a very fast pace. This means that a Six Sigma organization does not have the luxury of spending years to research a problem before coming up with a decision. For the management of a Six Sigma company, it is important to determine how much information is useful enough to take a course of action. As soon as the management is confident that what they have is good enough to make a decision, the project has to move from the *Analyze* to the *Improve* stage, or *Improve* to *Control* stage. Though the organization would have discovered more opportunities if it had spent more time studying the information, the number of mistakes made are far less compared to the average traditional organization that does not use Six Sigma techniques.

The Tools of Six Sigma

There are many tools that can be used in Six Sigma. The list below takes into account some of the key methods used:

- Continuous improvement

- Change management

- Business process management

- Balanced scorecards

- Process management

- Root cause analysis

- Process design

- Voice of the customer

- Statistical process control

The Benefits of Six Sigma

If an organization is thriving and doing well, why would it want to apply Six Sigma methods? Why are so many businesses, ranging from the prominent to the modest, implementing this unconventional business approach? While some have tested the system and failed to achieve their goals, those organizations that have applied the Six Sigma approach properly have benefited immensely. There are several definite benefits to Six Sigma:

1. Six Sigma strengthens the organization and boosts its chances of survival and success. In order to prevail over challenging economic conditions, grow the organization, and hold on to shifting markets, it is important to continuously innovate. Six Sigma tools can be used to develop the skills and culture needed to survive and thrive.

2. Six Sigma gets everyone working toward the same performance goal. Whatever the size of the company, getting every employee to focus on a common goal is very

difficult. Since every unit within the organization works towards its own objectives, the only common thread is delivery of information, products, and services to customers. By focusing on the process and the customer, Six Sigma is able to develop a consistent goal – an almost perfect level of performance. The Six Sigma performance goal is set at 99.9997% perfect, which is a very high standard. However, if the 99% quality that most companies tout as a standard is used in comparison, the difference is staggering. For example, for every 100, 000 deliveries made by a company using the traditional 99% performance goal, there would be 1000 incorrect deliveries. If the same company would adopt the Six Sigma performance goal of 99.9997%, there would be only 1 incorrect delivery!

3. Six Sigma prioritizes value for customers. Most organizations have admitted that Six Sigma has improved their perspective of what value means to customers. Even though an organization may be the best in its field, performance is often far removed from customer expectations. Six Sigma focuses on delivering value to customers profitably.

4. Six Sigma boosts performance and improves the rate of improvement. There is no organization that does not want to improve every day. Yet the attempts made usually fail to deliver the desired results demanded by the market. Six Sigma adopts tools and concepts from numerous disciplines in order to establish a foundation that will accelerate performance and improvement.

5. Six Sigma creates a learning organization. An organization where the employees are constantly learning

will always find itself able to generate new ideas that accelerate innovation and development. Workers with experience in a specific field can be transferred to different sector within the company, taking with them fresh ideas and better application methods. Six Sigma promotes learning and cross-pollination so that rather than focusing on differences in ideas between sectors, people can work together to achieve common goals.

Six Sigma is not a new approach to doing business. It is an effective and efficient way for an organization to focus on providing quality products and services to customers, and profits for its owners. On its own, Six Sigma is a great way to manage a business, but combine it with the Lean philosophy and the results can be amazing. Let's see how these two philosophies can be merged to form Lean Six Sigma.

Chapter 4: The Principles of Lean Six Sigma

Every organization that does business and aims to make a profit has one main priority – *Customer Satisfaction*. For a company to succeed, it must have the ability to guarantee the best quality at the lowest cost. In the 80s, the traditional thinking had always been that it was too expensive to produce quality goods and services. However, Motorola came in with an entirely new way of thinking. The company decided that if they could produce products of higher quality, their cost of production would go down. Customer satisfaction was prioritized in order to realize greater profitability.

In today's world, the business environment does not tolerate errors. Lean Six Sigma is able to help any organization focus its energy on improving its business processes in order to boost profits and satisfy customer needs. It is, therefore, imperative for every organization to put into practice the principles of Lean Six Sigma.

The Key Principles of Lean Six Sigma

Lean Six Sigma principles revolve around delighting customers by providing better quality products and services in less time. In order to achieve this objective, the company must improve their processes. People must engage in activities aimed at eliminating defects and placing emphasis on making the flow throughout the work process smoother. Any organization that wants to stay ahead of its competitors must innovate continuously, and this requires teamwork and sharing ideas so that problems can be identified and resolved quickly.

All these elements must work together in harmony. Focusing on one element at the expense of the others is a recipe for failure. At the end of the day, all these elements are fundamentally dependent on the collection of facts and data. Here are the seven principles of Lean Six Sigma in detail:

1. Focus on the customer.
This is also known as the law of the market. The customer must always be prioritized when it comes to producing goods or delivering services. This should be a non-negotiable principle that ever employee needs to adhere to. The company must make it clear to everyone that if there were no customers, there would be no business. The organization must focus on delighting its customers with speed and quality.

There used to be a time when employees used to believe that the only person who was entitled to an opinion was the CEO. It was the boss who decided what constituted a quality product or service. Nowadays, such traditional ways of thinking have been discarded and new attitudes adopted. It is now clear that the customer is the only one who defines quality. It is customers who buy the products and services, and they are always comparing what a company offers to alternatives within the market. A customer will only buy a company's product if it suits their needs. This is why every Lean Six Sigma project begins by attempting to find out what attributes customers focus on when they compare different companies. The companies that deliver quality are the ones who take the time to look into the marketplace through the eyes of their customers.

In order to satisfy customers, the first goal should be to get rid of anything that does not meet their requirements. Such things are referred to as defects. Once the company knows what the customers need, the next step is to determine if those needs have been met. If not, then defects are being produced in the process. Another issue that needs to be addressed is the speed of delivery. If a process is slow, there is a higher chance of producing defects. Any kind of unnecessary delays or waiting time, where an item sits as it waits to be worked on, should be eliminated.

Customers can be external as well as internal. Internal customers are the people within the organization who receive work from others. Their input also deserves to be considered when defining quality. The concept of *Voice of the Customer*, or VOC, is used to signify that customer's needs and opinions are being taken into consideration during the decision-making process. VOC techniques may include creating focus groups, tracking complaints, or visiting customer websites.

2. Identify and understand the value stream
There is an old saying that says, "If you don't know where you are going, any road will take you there." One of the most

critical steps of the Lean Six Sigma discipline is analyzing the value stream in order to first determine where the organization is supposed to go. There are three questions that must be asked before the value stream can be identified and understood:

- What is value?

- What is the value stream?

- What is the significance of a value stream?

All organizations are engaged in activities that are geared towards producing and delivering goods or services for customers. Therefore, value is whatever the customers are ready to pay for. A value stream is the whole collection of those activities that enable the product to reach the customer. The value stream is significant because it helps the company understand the actions it is taking as part of its business process.

The goal of identifying and understanding the value stream is to find ways of separating value-adding activities from those that do not create value for the customer. Once the value stream has been analyzed from beginning to end, an organization will be able to eliminate activities that do not add value, while also identifying opportunities for process improvement. This will, in turn, boost profitability.

How does an organization identify its value streams? The first step is to group its products or services into families, where possible. The second step is to choose one product or service family and analyze its value stream. This can be done using criteria such as products with the most customer returns, products with the most defects, or products with the highest volume. The final step is to walk backward through the value stream, beginning from the customer to the supply of materials.

3. Improve and smooth the process flow

Improving and smoothing the flow of a process requires some flexibility. A work process should be designed in a way that makes it easy to maneuver and work with. It is important that there be progressive achievement of activities in the value stream. This enables the product or service to start from the design phase to the delivery phase with no backflows, scrap, or stoppages. The aim is a continuous flow.

The steps in the process that do not add value should be removed. It is also important not to overproduce items or push them through too early before customers need them. This might create bottlenecks and waste.

4. Eliminate waste and useless steps

If a process involves too many steps and most of these steps are not really adding value to the final output, then there is probably some waste (*muda*) being produced. One tool that is used to analyze the value stream is the *Value Added Flow Chart*. This tool enables the total value stream to be divided into two categories: value adding and non-value adding activities. The flow chart helps to discover priorities for improvement.

Another useful tool is the *Value Stream Map*, which is used to provide greater details to process improvement efforts. This tool is used to help an organization focus its team efforts on specific waste elimination projects. In order to achieve this goal, it is crucial to first create a map of the current state of the value stream, followed by a second map showing the future state of the value stream. The end result should be the development of specific action plans for supporting the improvement of the value stream.

5. Manage using data and minimize variation

Before an organization jumps to conclusions on what its problems are and how to resolve them, there has to be an examination of the facts. The right metrics have to be measured the right way. Collecting data is a precise process and must be handled properly. Control Charts can be used to interpret data and understand variations in the process. This will guide the decision-makers on when to take specific actions and when not to.

6. Engage and equip employees

In order for the organization to attain operational excellence every day, the employees must feel that their input matters. The managers and team leaders must realize that they cannot achieve continuous improvement without involving and equipping the people in the processes. The employees need to feel empowered enough to challenge and enhance the process.

7. Perform systematic improvement activities

The DMAIC and DMADV frameworks are used to help the organization get the right data to improve the process. DMAIC is used to improve existing processes while DMADV is used when designing new processes.

What is DMAIC?

The simplest way to look at Lean Six Sigma is to view it as a problem-solving process. This process is made up of five phases known by the acronym DMAIC – Define, Measure, Analyze, Improve, and Control. DMAIC is a management system that helps in generating a constant stream of projects that require improvement. Every business faces obstacles to its operations, and Lean Six Sigma offers guidelines that enable selection of the right projects at the right time. Once this is achieved, DMAIC is used to filter the projects further and deliver results that are quantifiable and sustainable results.

Phases of DMAIC

Define
This is the initial phase of Lean Six Sigma. The project leaders come up with a project charter, develop a high-level view of the process, and try to understand customer needs. The team needs to create an outline that will guide their efforts. This outline includes defining the problem, the goals, the process, and the customer.

When defining the problem, it is necessary to come up with a problem statement. First, there should be some data that highlights the existence of a problem within the process. Then the team should verify that the problem is of high priority and is likely to have a great impact if not resolved. Finally, it should be ascertained whether the organization has enough resources to solve the issue.

Defining the goal statement involves defining measurable and time-bound terms of what project success will look like. Defining the process is done by creating maps that help the team decide on the critical areas that need to be looked into. Defining the customer and their needs involves contacting them to understand their needs. This will provide the team with information that will help solve the problem.

Measure
This involves quantifying the problem. It is important to constantly measure the process, with the team leaders focusing on the collection of data. The first step is to establish the current performance of the process. This is known as the "baseline," and is the standard of measure. It should be in place before any changes are made. The second step is to determine the cause of the problem or waste by reviewing the data collected. The team must create a detailed data collection plan where they will consider where to obtain the data, how much to collect, and who is responsible for this task. It is important that the team collects data that is reliable rather than make assumptions. Finally, the team should update the project charter. By the end of this phase, there should be more information about process performance, goals, and problems.

Analyze
This involves identifying the root cause of the problem. The team that collects the data may be split according to the different types of data required. The review team analyzes the data collected during the Measure phase and may choose to include more information. The aim is to find the root causes of defects and waste.

In this phase, it is important to closely inspect the value of each step in the process by engaging in *Process Analysis*. The team should brainstorm the probable causes of waste, defects, and lost time. Prior to moving on to the Improve phase, the causes of the problem should be double-checked. Once additional data has been obtained, the project charter should be updated.

Improve

This phase involves solution development, which should be done after all the data has been collected and analyzed accordingly. The aim should be to generate as many ideas as possible in order to pick the best one out of all. The team will then create maps that will help in visualizing the potential solutions and how these solutions will resolve issues of waste, rework loops, and delays. The best solution is then chosen and implemented. It is also important to measure the improvement that results from the new solution prior to moving to the Control phase.

Control

This phase involves sustaining the new solution. The control phase is similar to process management, and the team involved starts to document how the employees within the process will access and utilize the new infrastructure. It is important to note that the process must continuously be improved and it should never be assumed that control is a one-off event. This means that the team responsible for developing the new solution must identify a few parameters that will be monitored throughout. This should go hand in hand with a response plan in case problems arise. There should also be adequate documentation of the relevant checklists, process maps, etc. This new knowledge can also be used to improve processes in other areas of the organization. Finally, every successful project needs to end in sharing and celebration.

Part II: Preparing For Lean Six Sigma

Chapter 5: Knowing Who Your Customers Are

The majority of companies that refuse to adopt Lean Six Sigma as a strategy to improve their business processes tend to make the excuse that it is too complex for them. The claim made is that they simply do not have the resources to develop an infrastructure and train employees. These companies go to the extent of saying that Lean Six Sigma is a burden that would only slow down their processes and prevent them from meeting customer needs.

What they fail to realize is that, most likely, they are not really satisfying the demands of their own customers because they are ignorant of their customer's true needs. An organization generally has different classes of customers, such as end users, dealers, employees, management, et cetera. Knowing and understanding the customers is vital to the profitability of an organization. Therefore, every organization that seeks to improve their processes and give their customers what they need must adopt an organized approach toward this.

Who are the customers, really?

There are three critical factors that an organization must consider in order to determine who their true customers are:

1. **The primary customer** – Most companies tend to believe that their distributor is their primary customer. Nothing could be farther from the truth. The end-consumer has needs and requirements that must be taken care of. If not, the company will suffer as demand for their products and services will drop. This doesn't mean that the distributor should not be taken into consideration as a customer. The distributor is also crucial to the process since they are responsible for pushing the company's product. However, the truth is that if the end-consumer is satisfied with a company, the distributor will automatically benefit.

2. **The congruency of the pain points of different customers** – Customers may have needs that are similar, while other needs may not be congruent. It is important for a company to understand where these similarities and differences in pain points lie. For example, a dealer may be more interested in transaction efficiency while the end user may require more education and guidance. These are two distinct pain points that a company must address. The company should measure the impact of each pain point on its revenue stream and then prioritize accordingly.

3. **The worth of the customer** – It is true that one end-customer can never be equated to one dealer or distributor. On the other hand, the dealer will only be happy if the end-customer is also happy. An angry end-user who is not satisfied with a company's products or services can cost the dealer a lot of money and time. If the dealer is selling several different brands, they may be forced recommend rival brands. This can result in huge financial losses for a company, especially if considered from a long-term financial perspective. The company needs to ask itself which customers have the greatest worth.

Grouping the Customers

One of the best ways for a company to recognize the different requirements of their customers is to segment them into groups. This helps in developing products and services that suit the requirements of each group. It also enables the company to develop measures that will specifically address performance issues relating to each group's requirements. Listed below are some of the categories that a company may use to segment their customers – the past, present, or future:

- Spend

- Price sensitivity

- End use

- Size

- Age

- Gender

- Geographical location

- Loyalty

- Frequency of purchase

- Industry

- Buying characteristics

- Impact

- Socio-economic factors

Of course, an organization will choose which categories are most applicable to its operations, but the list above is a good place to start.

Understanding the Customer Process

The first step in developing an organized approach to understanding the customer process is creating a customer strategy. Most companies think that they already have a solid customer strategy, such as a large budget for the sales department. However, this is a weak customer strategy that does not really help the company understand the customer process. So what is the best approach to take in order to understand the customer process?

There are three ways through which managers and team leaders can outline and document the organization's customer strategy. These are:

1. Developing business architecture

The aim of creating business architecture is to help everyone within the organization visualize and understand how every department is linked to the various customers the business has. The problem with a traditional company is that the workers cannot see how their everyday activities affect other departments much less how their work affects customers. For a Lean Six Sigma company, business architecture is one of the best ways to resolve this.

In order to understand business architecture, people must be able to view it graphically. It needs to be represented in a diagram that shows how customers are linked to business processes. It must be noted that these processes are not the same thing as the departments within the company.

There are five key ways of determining whether a company has developed functional business architecture:

- The architecture is simple enough to fit into a one-page diagram.

- Every department within the organization is represented in the picture.

- The architecture links together departments into processes that customers care about.

- Every individual in the company can draw a line-of-sight from the work they do all the way to the customer.

- The architecture focuses more on how the company plans to satisfy customer needs so as to achieve its goals than how business is currently being conducted.

It is not necessary to reorganize the organization chart to fit into the business architecture. There is no problem if a company chooses to do so. However, reorganizing can sometimes create distractions that do not help in providing the customers with what they need. A business architecture is simply designed to graphically describe how everyone is linked together to serve customers.

Developing business architecture makes it easier for other kinds of work processes to flow. Once it is in place, customer research can be steered in the right direction. Products can be evaluated to determine how effective they are in providing value for customers. Funds can be channeled towards the processes that need it. Measures for solving problems can be refined to suit the business architecture.

Clear and easily understandable business architecture can speed up the rate at which organizational goals are achieved. It is the foundation for most of the management programs being used today.

2. Developing a Hoshin Plan

Hoshin can be translated into "compass." It is a strategic planning process that involves an organization setting its direction and aligning available resources to meet long-term goals. Hoshin planning is very effective in formulating and executing strategies for meeting customer needs and attaining shareholder goals. It documents the approach and 12-month performance plan of an organization. A Hoshin plan includes the following elements:

Deploying objectives:
- Establishing key metrics at the executive level.

- Deciding on the customer, financial, and operations metrics to support strategic objectives.

- Narrowing the key metrics in order to focus on the few critical ones.

- Agreeing on how measures will be taken and reported.

- Reviewing performance every week.

Selecting Key Projects:
- Ensuring that all key projects are linked to the Hoshin plan.

- Ensuring that a project is not undertaken simply as a "cost avoidance" measure. Every project must show evidence of bringing about improvement inproductivity, income savings, or customer delight.

- Reviewing projects at an executive level every month to determine progress toward objectives.

- Focusing on measurable progress during reviews and ensuring financial resources are available in advance.

- Celebrating project success and moving on.

3. Developing Information, Process and Infrastructure diagram

The role of an information, process and infrastructure (IPI) diagram is to elevate the business architecture and Hoshin planning strategies by painting an accurate picture of present and future business environments. An IPI diagram is created through a process that is dynamic and iterative. The common practice is to use DMAIC tools to get information and documentation, create the drawings, and verify these drawings to make sure they precisely represent the present and future environment.

One of the foundational elements of an IPI diagram is the SIPOC (Supplier, Input, Process, Output, and Customer) diagram, which is simply a diagram that depicts what an organization does to meet customer needs. Another building block of an IPI diagram is the value stream map, which helps to determine which steps add value and which ones don't, according to the customer's perspective.

A customer strategy process that is well defined should always be supported by the business architecture, Hoshin plan, and IPI diagram. A customer-centric company should always be looking for ways to enhance customer experience while accelerating growth and generating profits.

Chapter 6: Understanding Customer Needs

Customer needs are always changing. Some of the products or services that people thought were useful yesterday are not even in the market today. In most cases, the customers do not even realize that their own needs have changed, and are pleasantly surprised when companies come up with new and more advanced products.

The Kano Model

This is a powerful technique that was created by Noriaki Kano, a professor at Tokyo Rika University. The Kano analysis helps a company analyze its customer's needs and how it can identify customer requirements. According to Kano's model, customer satisfaction is directly proportional to the level of functionality that a product or service has.

The Kano model focuses on satisfying three kinds of needs:

Basic needs – Satisfying these needs enable a company to enter a market. Basic needs are the expected characteristics that a product or service has. Basic needs are not usually spoken because the customer considers them to be obvious. If these needs are not met, extreme dissatisfaction sets in. For example, a clean table and cutlery are basic needs in a restaurant. The customer does not need to ask for a clean table. It is an expectation.

Performance needs – Satisfying these needs enables a company to stay in the market. Performance needs are the standard features that elevate or reduce satisfaction depending on their scale, such as price or speed. These needs are usually spoken by the customer, for example requesting WIFI access or a table in the non-smoking section.

Excitement needs – Satisfying these needs enable a company to become world class. They include the unexpected features that customers are impressed with and are not usually spoken. For example, free freshly baked cookies being delivered to a customer's hotel room during turndown service.

How customer requirements can be identified

Basic customer needs can be identified using the following techniques:

- Complaint systems

- Attrition analysis

- Internal quality process measures
- Win/Loss reports

Performance needs can be identified using the following

techniques:

- Customer satisfaction surveys

- Focus groups

- Transactional reports

- Perceptual surveys

Excitement needs can be identified using the following techniques:

- Customer loyalty programs

- "Invent-the-future" focus programs

- "Leading edge" forums

The Kano model helps a company to recognize the customer's unspoken needs so that they can be prioritized. To get the most out of the Kano analysis, it should be incorporated into the company's multi-generational project plan. While it is obvious that the basic needs must be the first to be provided, the company must also understand that customer expectation varies over time. The cookies freely offered may have been popular in the past, but people are more health conscious today. Offering free WIFI is no longer a performance or excitement need but a basic one. Customer needs change.

Voice of the Customer (VOC)

Voice of the Customer refers to the customer's comments, expectations, or preferences regarding a product or service. It is a process that companies use to gather feedback from customers in order to provide them with quality products and services. There are two ways of categorizing customers:

- Internal customers – These are customers who exist within an organization. They include management, employees, or departments inside an organization.

- External customers – These are customers who exist outside the organization. They are the end-users of the products or services or have some kind of vested interest in the organization. They include end-customers, clients, and shareholders.

The organization must be constantly proactive and innovating so that it stays abreast of the changing customer needs and requirements. Needs are the desires or expectations that a customer has regarding a product or service. Requirements are the attributes a product or service has that help satisfy that need.

Voice of Customer can either be spoken (current) or unspoken (latent). The VOC methodology is used to capture the needs of the customer via verbatim comments. Through VOC, an organization is able to translate the customer's comments into customer needs, and then incorporate that information to produce products and services that meet customer requirements.

Categories of VOC
From an organizational perspective, VOC is categorized into four broad classes, commonly referred to as AICP:

- Voice of Associate – Feedback received from employees.

- Voice of Investor – Feedback received from shareholders and management.

- Voice of Customer – Feedback received from end-consumers and clients.

- Voice of Process – Feedback received after measuring CTQs (Critical-To-Quality) and CTPs (Critical-To-Process).

VOC Methods

Feedback from customers can be obtained through different techniques, such as:

- Direct interviews – These are one-on-one meetings with existing or potential customers. The interviewer asks questions and the answers are discussed to better understand the customer's viewpoint.

- Observations – Customer behavior or response to products or services is observed and feedback is obtained.

- Focus groups – This is a group of individuals who are brought together in one room to discuss specific topics related to a product or service. Focus groups are perfect for identifying CTQs (Critical-To-Quality). The information received, however, cannot be generalized.

- Surveys – These are questionnaires containing a set of questions that are sent to customers. Though they are popular due to their cost effectiveness, surveys generally have a poor response rate.

- Suggestions – The opinions of customers are collected and examined to see whether they are useful for improving products or services. Though suggestions provide good information for product improvement, they are limited in terms of the overall production process.

Advancements in VOC: Understanding Customers Better

The majority of companies that claim to use VOC data in their decision-making generally use VOC methods as in the following ways:

- Observations – 18%

- Surveys – 65%

- Focus groups – 53%

- Product/service testing – 50%

The fact of the matter is that these figures paint a sad state of affairs if a company is to beat its competitors. Most of the traditional VOC methods of collecting data are not as reliable as required. If a company is planning on pushing its market boundaries in the future by using these VOC methods, it will not succeed. Another factor to consider is that most companies aren't really making good use of existing VOC methods anyway. Yet it is clear that the company that understands the market and its customers best will be the last man standing.

As time passes, traditional VOC methods just won't be enough. Customers often are unable to explain their needs in a way that would help a company create transformational or innovative products and services. There are a number of reasons for this:

- Customers are generally unaware of a company's capabilities. They do not realize that a company may be able to solve a problem that they have.

- Customers only show creativity when it comes to their own jobs rather than on products or services used.

- Customers tend to be good at reacting to a specific idea but stumble when asked to come up with their own.

- Customers often lie when asked about how much they like a new product. They may not want to offend or start an argument.

Asking customers what they like or what improvements they need is not the best way to improve a process, product, or service. So then, what is the best way? *Customer ethnography*!

Customer Ethnography
The answer lies in making close observations of customers and incorporating their behavior into the design of a product or service. This is known as ethnography. Ethnography is the systematic study of a group of people in their natural setting. It is a social anthropology discipline that involves trying to

understand how people in a society live in their natural, real-world environment.

A company has to find a way to integrate itself into the lives of selected customers in order to better understand their needs and the way they use products and services in real life. The simplest way to do this would be direct observation of customers. The aim would be to recognize things that would potentially make life easier for them.

Ethnography is meant to generate an intuitive understanding of a customer's needs and dissatisfactions in a way that automatically inspires creative solutions. To do this, a company should pick about 10 of its existing or potential customers. Unlike traditional VOC methods that rely heavily on large numbers of participants, ethnography is more concerned with quality. The company should then hire a team of trained personnel to observe the customers. The aims should be to:

- Establish a holistic perspective of customer needs. Every single behavior or activity associated with a specific need, product or service is noted.

- Recognize and note down things that customers do subconsciously.

- Identify any frustrations the customer has, whether it is linked to the company's product or not.

Ethnography has the potential to help any organization develop deeper insights into customer behavior and needs. It can even ignite innovations in a product or service. As with any other data collection method in use, there are a few downsides. Ethnography is time-consuming and labor intensive. A company should also be careful not to depend on just a small sample of customers when designing or improving a product or service. After an ethnographic study, it is recommended that the traditional VOC methods be used to verify the findings.

Critical To Quality (CTQ) Requirements

Once VOC information regarding the generic needs of customers has been collected, it is time to translate these needs into precise items known as Critical-To-Quality requirements. CTQs are internal quality constraints that are linked to the needs of the customer. They are critical to the quality of a product, service, or process, and are necessary for ensuring that the customer's needs are satisfied.

By writing the CTQs in a measurable and specific form, it will be possible for the organization to create a process measurement set. The role of this set is to help in establishing the appropriate measures for assessing process performance. In order to know if the CTQs are specific enough, the question must be asked, "Is it possible to write a detailed operational definition or formula to effectively describe the customers' needs?" The needs must be detailed enough to allow the company to align improvement activities with customer requirements. It is not the job of a CTQ to provide a solution. It is only a measurement that may sometimes define the upper and lower limits, as well as a target value.

In order to translate the VOC information into specific CTQs, the broad needs of internal and external customers should be considered. Three generic needs include:

- Cost – This requires the assessment of the efficiency of a company's operating processes. The cost of producing the output should be considered.

- Time – Do the customers get the product or service when they want it?

- Quality – Did the product or service reach the customer? Did it meet specifications?

It is also important to first differentiate between the characteristics of the product and of the process. The customer is usually more interested in the product characteristics satisfying their needs rather than the process characteristics. The organization is usually more likely to look at things from the process characteristics perspective. This is why it is important for the organization to ask its customers some questions. The questions need to be clear and the answers should be refined continuously until precise and measurable data is obtained. This questioning process can be explained using the example below.

The manager of a hotel wants to know what customers consider to be most important about their hotel rooms. After asking a few questions, the customer feedback is quite generic. Most say that they prefer a "good hotel room." This is the first CTQ requirement for the hotel's customers, but the answer is so vague, it doesn't do much good. The hotel manager will have to figure out what "good" actually means by asking customers to give more specific information. The customers respond by clarifying that a good hotel room means:

- A clean room

- A room with Hi-Speed internet

- A hotel with a gym

- A room with a TV that has many channels

At this point, if the hotel manager can come up with a metric or formula for measuring these product/service characteristics, they may be one step closer to defining what customers truly need. If not, the process must be repeated until every need has been specified in a measurable way. The hotel manager has to look at each room or hotel characteristic and develop an appropriate metric. For example:

- A clean room – Clean sheets and towels, clean bathroom, no garbage in the wastebasket.

- A room with Hi-Speed Internet – Number of rooms having Hi-Speed Internet.

- A hotel with a gym – Number of hours the gym is open every day.

- A room with a TV that has many channels – Number of functioning channels every day.

So far, the hotel manager has done a good job establishing measurable metrics for the last three customer needs. However, the first need is still undefined. The metrics below can be used with the first customer need:

- Clean sheets and towels – Number of days between sheet and towel changes.

- Clean bathroom – Needs further refining to develop a metric.

- No garbage in waste basket – Number of rooms with full wastebaskets every day

All CTQs have been stated in specific and measurable terms. The customer need that is still pending needs to be taken through the process again until it can be measured objectively. The next phase would be to identify those needs that customers really care about. The needs of the business may not always align with the needs of the customers. These conflicts must be rationalized.

Part III: Implementing Lean Six Sigma

Chapter 7: Getting Top Management Support

It is absolutely critical that top management is fully onboard prior to beginning a Lean Six Sigma program. However, there are some instances where improvement efforts are driven by lower or mid-level managers rather than the top brass. The top management may be unwilling to invest the time and money to improve processes when there are many financial pressures to be dealt with. This may make it very difficult for the process improvement measures to spread throughout the entire organization. There are two approaches towards turning top management reluctance into support for Lean Six Sigma initiatives:

- Stealth approach

- Limited Initial Commitment approach

Stealth Approach

This is where some managers or departments begin implementing Lean Six Sigma on a small-scale under the radar. The aim is to actualize significant benefits of improving processes while keeping a low profile. There are a number of variations to this approach but the general technique is as described below:

1. **Identification and clear articulation of the gap that separates actual and desired process performance**. This should be done by a small (1 to 3) core group of people who believe in the mission to improve the process. It is recommended that at least one of these individuals be knowledgeable about Lean Six Sigma. This step should take about 2 days.

2. **Articulation of the needs for the project.** The group should come up with reasons why the improvement is beneficial to the organization. These could be financial and customer reasons. They could also be emotional reasons, such as reduced job frustration, workmanship pride, or getting rid of bureaucracy. This should not take more than 3 days

3. **Utilization of project selection criteria to assess potential projects**. These criteria include quick payback, the high potential for success, business strategy support, availability of data, and a self-contained process that won't require arbitration from senior management. The team should also consider adding other criteria that will highlight the value of Lean Six Sigma to management. This step should take around 2 days.

4. **Completion of project organization**. A champion should be selected to resolve any minor political battles. Every team member should receive training. This should take 1 to 2 days.

5. **Addressing of the problem using DMAIC where suitable.** It should be noted that focus is to be placed on achievement of quick results rather than adherence to the methodology. For example, the team should pick simple Lean Six Sigma principles and tools like waste elimination, check sheets, and Pareto charts. Complex and lengthy tools like FMEA should be avoided. If DMAIC is used, the team must not take too much time undertaking the DMA phases. This step should include 4 additional people on top of the core group and must take no more than 5 weeks.

6. **Presentation of results.** Top management is shown the results and a request is made for implementation of Lean Six Sigma throughout the organization.

Limited Initial Commitment Approach

The goal of this approach is to fix a number of problems that are of interest to top leadership and demonstrate improvement quickly. If this is done, it will be easier for senior management to commit to a broad rollout of Lean Six Sigma in the organization. The steps for this approach include:

1. **Engaging with top management to identify around 2-4 problems or opportunities.** The team should consist of three core members, with one of them

being knowledgeable in Lean Six Sigma. This should take 1-5 days.

2. **Collaboratively developing criteria for project selection and then establishing three projects that meet these criteria**. Some of these criteria include: supporting the business strategy, supporting a minimum of one senior management problem, rapid payback, readily available data, high potential for success, and easy establishment of milestones for the long-term projects. This step should involve the core team as well as top management. This should take 1-4 days.

3. **Finalizing of project organization**. Some mid-level managers and frontline employees should be involved and trained accordingly. This should take 1-5 days.

4. **Identifying the critical stakeholders and creating ways to get them to commit to the success of the team.** This should involve the core group and about 15 others who will be split into three sub-teams. This can take 1-3 days.

5. **Where appropriate, DMAIC should be used to address the problem.** As before, the focus should be on rapid achievement of results and not adherence to the methodology. This activity should take 2-9 weeks.

6. **Conducting regular status checks to make sure of project progress and financial gains.** If progress has been made, interim celebrations should be conducted and gifts (cash bonuses, stock options, etc.) awarded. This step involves the improvement team and top

management. The status checks are to be conducted throughout the project.

7. **Presentation of final results** to senior management and subsequent roll-out of Lean Six Sigma organization-wide.

It should be noted that the Limited Initial Commitment approach is not the same as the Pilot approach. Firstly, unlike the pilot approach, this approach has active top management involvement throughout. Secondly, this approach is intended to generate further interest in improving the processes, and therefore the initial "fixes" are not supposed to be final. Finally, this approach includes a mini-portfolio of diverse projects and Lean Six Sigma tools rather than just a single project. Pilot projects are not as versatile in terms of fixing different problem situations.

How to Overcome Top Management Reluctance for Lean Six Sigma

1. Ensure rapid results – The benefits of the project must be seen quickly and exceed costs. The team should try to maintain a timeframe of five weeks maximum and a 30% minimum return. The aim is to turn the heads of top management, show an ability to keep costs low and generate momentum for future improvement.

2. Use good project selection criteria – This will help the team pick the best projects possible and demonstrate value to top management.

3. Define project scope well – The scope should be narrow enough to ensure fast completion and broad enough to bring real benefits. The team members must keep their eyes fixed on the original project goals to avoid scope creep.

4. Set own goals – A team that sets its own goals will find it easier to stay motivated and committed to the successful completion of projects, despite the daily pressures of work.

5. Get Lean Six Sigma experts – The team must find people, whether internally or externally, who understand how to use Lean Six Sigma principles. This will increase the chances of deployment throughout the organization.

6. Monitor interim progress – It is important to create a work plan that has key milestones, clear deliverables, and allocates responsibilities. This will ensure fast and high-quality results.

7. Target processes that are people-intensive rather than machine -intensive – Improvement projects that involve a lot of people tend to bear faster results because humans have greater variability than machines. People will not do the same task the same way all the time, and different people will perform the same task in different ways. It will be easier to make quick gains in processes that tend to be people-oriented than machine or chemical-driven.

8. Create conducive team atmosphere – The way team members interact with one another has a big effect on project success. The project leaders must be able to

regularly bring teams together to improve working relationships.

Tips for Ensuring Lean Six Sigma Works for the Organization

1. Secure top management commitment. The senior managers must first be trained by introducing them to Lean Six Sigma. They must be convinced that it is beneficial to the organization.

2. Train and educate all leaders to become Lean Six Sigma Champions. The Champions should include functional managers, process owners, and the steering committee.

3. Incorporate Lean Six Sigma into the company's next business operating plan.

4. Choose training consultants who have practiced Lean Six Sigma rather than those who only know how to teach theory. Get the right consultants for the Belts.

5. Involve employees on the shop floor. Instead of a few Green or Black Belts doing all the projects, train supervisors, and shop floor operators how to use the appropriate tools and techniques. Start a White Belt program to motivate them to start projects of their own.

6. Create a mentoring program where the experienced practitioners help the new trainees. This ensures that projects are finished on time and regular course corrections are made.

7. Ensure that the returns are at least 20 times the training investment. Defining the project well and allocating the right practitioners will help achieve this.

8. Validate the financial metrics of all projects. The finance leader should verify any financial savings that accrue from the project, and the finance department must check the metrics during the control phase.

9. Start a thorough and genuine certification process. Once a candidate successfully completes a project and displays an ability to use tools and techniques properly, they should get certified. The certificate should be signed by the Lean Six Sigma reviewer, the finance leader, and the functional manager.

10. Lean Six Sigma should not be defined as the responsibility of the quality manager. The job of the quality manager is generally very distinct and they cannot be tasked with managing Lean Six Sigma for the entire organization.

Chapter 8: Deployment Planning

Deploying Lean Six Sigma is a decision that has to be taken seriously. Tough questions must be asked and answered before taking those critical first steps. One of the first steps that have to be taken is creating a plan that addresses the key issues affecting organizational processes. The executives and leaders must also consider potential challenges that may be faced.

The Decision to Deploy

The level of success of Lean Six Sigma initiatives will depend on whether certain conditions are met. Before a deployment decision is made, there are a few questions that need to be asked:

1. Are there any compelling reasons for Lean Six Sigma deployment?

Every Lean Six Sigma initiative experiences initial deployment obstacles. Having a simple, convincing, and motivating reason for deployment will generate the energy necessary to break through these obstacles. Most people within the organization will not be easily convinced of the need to change the status quo. Therefore, there has to be a really good reason to convince people to get on board.

Compelling reasons could include the organization suffering huge quality losses, poor customer satisfaction, or even new rivals entering and dominating the market. A burning platform is a great way to motivate people to embrace a continuous improvement initiative.

2. What are the explicit goals of the initiative?

A burning platform is a great way to develop the push required to deploy Lean Six Sigma. However, it is also necessary to develop a pull. This pull comes in the form of goals that are specific and designed to show how the organization will look in the future. These goals should highlight the business case for Lean Six Sigma and may include:

- Fundamental change in business culture and management.

- Effective conversion of strategy into results.

- Solving problems throughout the organization.

- Reduction of costs while improving customer satisfaction.

- Increasing revenues.

It is critical that management agrees on the goals before deployment in order to make planning easier and avoid false starts.

3. Is top management strongly supportive of the initiative?

Leadership has no substitute. There must be high-level executive involvement in order to steer the deployment process, hold managers accountable, and tear down any organizational barriers. The executive who is sponsoring the initiative must be determined and willing to sacrifice to make Lean Six Sigma work.

4. Will Lean Six Sigma resolve the problems plaguing the organization?

Most organizations tend to believe that Lean Six Sigma is the solution to all their problems. However, there are certain issues that this initiative simply cannot fix. If the organization is faced with bad leadership, financial restructuring, or a poor business strategy, then Lean Six Sigma isn't the answer. It may provide the tools to understand and improve the process capability of the organization, but some underlying issues have to be fixed separately before deployment.

Internal Customer Requirements for Deployment

In most business processes, the customer always comes first. Deployment is no different. It is the customer's ability to see the solution to their need and pay for it that determines the value of deployment. It is, therefore, important to understand internal customer requirements when using Lean Six Sigma tools.

One way of accomplishing this is by creating a Critical-To

(CT) tree. This will enable the organization to refine its general deployment goals into precise and measurable performance specifications. A CT tree is developed using the following steps:

- Identification of deployment customers. These are people within the organization who decide to allocate resources toward Lean Six Sigma or have the authority to influence such decisions.

- Establishment of a rigorous and structured process to understand customer requirements. This can be done through focus groups or interviews.

- Obtaining measures and specifications. This involves determining how much money the initiative will save the organization and the time frame for doing so.

- Clarification of what a culture change means to the customer and ways of measuring it.

A CT tree helps to provide the necessary clarity and gain solid top management support. It is usually easy to get people to agree to something if it is vaguely described. Once the process has been clearly specified and measured, however, everyone knows exactly what they are getting into. This avoids misunderstandings, assumptions, and hidden agendas. In the end, it is much easier to design a deployment plan if expectations are clear.

Choosing a Deployment Model

A deployment model refers to the structure, scale, scope, and focus of the deployment. There are many models that can be used, but it is recommended that the model chosen be appropriate for that particular organization. There are four general deployment models, each highlighting issues that need to be addressed:

Organization-wide model

This is the traditional model used by most organizations. It requires a strong central management and is driven by top leadership. Every sector of the organization is involved and results are rapidly produced. It is easy to improve multiple functions at once since they are all involved. Deployment obstacles are easily broken down by strong top management, and the business can be transformed due to the model's scale and scope.

The biggest problem with this model is that there has to be strong, focused, and persistent leadership. These are features that are usually rare in the majority of organizations. There must also be a committed deployment team. This model is resource-intensive and other initiatives may suffer. It can be very challenging to execute.

The organization-wide model has been proven to be the most sustainable and with the greatest impact. If there is a powerful and committed leadership, and the deployment is done quickly and comprehensively, there will be enough momentum to override the resistance to change that plagues most organizations.

Business unit model

In this model, Lean Six Sigma is deployed in only one particular business unit of an organization. It is less complex than an organization-wide model as it requires a smaller and simpler infrastructure to support functions like project monitoring and training. Due to its size and nature, it is easier to get management to adopt it. This is a suitable model to use in organizations where people are very skeptical about Lean Six Sigma. Though it requires a strong business unit leader, it is not necessary to get executive support early on.

The disadvantage with the business unit model is that it does not really impact the organizational culture. It is also difficult for the deployment team to work across business units to improve processes. This model has to prove itself first before it can be transformed into an organization-wide initiative, which may take years. Finally, the people involved in the deployment team are only exposed to one business unit, thus limiting their ability to gain organization-wide experience.

Targeted model
In the targeted model, Lean Six Sigma is deployed to attack specific problems that may exist within one business unit or throughout the organization. It is a fast and effective model due to the ease of implementation. Due to the limited scale of the initiative, a lot of infrastructure is not needed and not many changes have to be made. The problems are the focal point and provide motivation for action. The targeted model is a good way of showing people the effectiveness of Lean Six Sigma.

On the other hand, this model is so narrowly focused that it cannot transform the business. Due to the fact that there isn't much infrastructure put in place to support this model, it becomes very difficult to later expand the initiative throughout the organization.

Grassroots model

This is where a few individuals in the lower ranks of the organization decide to deploy Lean Six Sigma to solve a specific problem. There is not much infrastructure support due to the scale and it is easy to start. If the localized initiative is successful, other parts of the organization may become interested in Lean Six Sigma.

The problem with this model is that it hardly ever leads to broader deployment. It is a guerilla style of deployment where top-level management is not involved and therefore resources are not made available. Since there is little infrastructure support, it is not easy to expand the narrow scope. Ultimately, the results obtained are usually very meager relative to the whole organization, thus making it very difficult to capture the attention of the top leadership.

Accountability for Deployment

It is extremely important to resolve accountability issues from the get go. Managers and executives must be held accountable for Lean Six Sigma results. If they are not made to be accountable, they are likely to marginalize the initiative. To improve accountability for results, the organization can link achievement of Lean Six Sigma goals to some form of significant compensation. This will reinforce accountability and ensure that resources are allocated where needed.

There must also be accountability for deployment execution. Someone must be held accountable for the procedures, policies, training, selection of Green and Black Belts, and project monitoring. These functions are best centralized to ensure efficiency. The individual responsible should report to a high-ranking executive, for example, CEO, in order to link the deployment to the organization's overall strategy.

Change Management

Mastering the tools of Lean Six Sigma is important, but what influences its success is the ability to manage change. People do not like it when the status quo is altered. All of a sudden, there is an emphasis on data rather than personal opinions, performance problems are brought to the fore, and process owners are forced to be accountable for improving the way they work.

This is why it is crucial to create a change management plan early. Quickly assess the stakeholders and their relevant departments and ask them the following questions:

- Is the value proposition for Lean Six Sigma well understood?

- Is the deployment plan understood?

- Do you support the Lean Six Sigma initiative?

- Do you have enough business knowledge and resources to support deployment?

Change management requires diplomacy and personal contact. Resistance can be rooted out if people feel that their opinions matter and have been taken into account. Even the most hardheaded stakeholders can be convinced if they are engaged early on.

Getting the Right Talent

The culture of the organization can be changed by taking a few high potential employees, training them as Black Belts for 1 – 3 years, and then unleashing them back into the workforce in leadership positions. They will then focus on applying Lean Six Sigma principles every day.

The challenge for most organizations is identifying who these high potential employees are, how to position them in leadership posts, and managing people's expectations and perceptions. There is also the fear that employees who are recognized as top performers might be poached by rival companies. The managers might also have differing opinions on what constitutes a top performer. The best way to overcome the numerous challenges of talent management is to work with the HR department from the onset to craft the relevant policies.

Maintaining Focus

Most management initiatives struggle to focus on the issues that matter the most. Think of a team that completes an improvement process only to learn that no one cared about the problem in the first place. Irrelevance is the greatest threat to a Lean Six Sigma initiative.

The deployment plan should always place emphasis on the relevant issues. Management should avoid focusing on small, mediocre and irrelevant projects just to keep the Black Belts busy. In order to keep Lean Six Sigma relevant, the right projects have to be selected. To identify which projects are most relevant, the top business goals must be taken into account.

It is important to undertake a Critical-To-Quality flow down in order to determine the transfer function $[Y = f(x)]$ and identify the dependencies for every business goal. This makes sure that there is a link between what top leadership cares about and the projects to be deployed. CTQ flow-down may be a simple idea but the execution is quite complex. Top managers must always be involved since they will help align the projects with the organization's strategies and goals. The process of identifying projects must be monitored by getting regular feedback from top executives. If the top leadership is excited about the project choices, it will show. Care should be taken to avoid a situation where they simply show interest out of obligation.

It Is Worth It

An organization can achieve great results by deploying Lean Six Sigma. Though there are some risks, they are not technical. The methodology, tools, and training are not complex enough to put off the initiative. What ultimately makes the difference between an impactful deployment and a failed management initiative is the ability to sort out issues of change management, leadership commitment, talent management, and accountability for results.

Chapter 9: Project Identification and Selection

Before a Lean Six Sigma project is deployed, the right projects have to be identified and selected. Most organizations are very good at selecting projects but do not adopt the proper techniques to identify the relevant projects. There are generally four preconditions that must be satisfied in order to identify as well as select a Lean Six Sigma project.

Step One: Understand the Organization's Strategic Plan

The deployment team must be totally familiar with the strategic plan of the organization. Strategic planning involves these steps:

- Developing a roadmap for accomplishing the strategic plan.

- Evaluating the stakeholder's interests.

- Formulating a mission statement using the input provided by the stakeholders.

- Creating a workable business model. This step should consider cultural as well as financial issues that result from the restructuring of current business lines. The addition of any new business lines should also be considered.

- Performance and financial auditing to gauge the organization's capabilities and fiscal muscle.

- Performing gap analysis in order to generate a list of gaps. This is done by comparing the present performance of the process with its desired state.

- Creating and implementing an action plan that will help accomplish organizational strategies while also closing any gaps.

- Developing contingency plans to take into consideration potential fluctuations in the market, pressure from competitors, and other situations that may affect the execution of the strategic plan.

- Deploying the plan throughout the organization. This can be achieved by establishing clear timeframes, measurable performance indices, and cascaded goals. The process owners must also be clearly identified.

Step Two: Align the Improvement Efforts with the Business Strategy

It is important for the project selection team to understand how the activities designed for process improvement should align with the strategic action plans. In Step One above, the team considered business modeling as a critical aspect of strategic planning. The team would most likely have analyzed and identified the Line of Business (LOB) and where it falls relative to the organization's competitive position and market growth. The objective is to find an effective strategy for a specific LOB based on the market growth rate and how competitive the LOB is.

For example, the organization's LOB may have a solid competitive position in a market that is growing very quickly. If this is the case, it would be best for the organization to prioritize product development rather than operations improvement. However, if the LOB has a weak competitive position in a market that is growing slowly, the organization should seriously consider using Lean Six Sigma to improve its cost structure.

Step Three: Incorporate the Action Plans into the Policy Deployment System

Policy deployment refers to cascading the goal-based plans of an organization throughout the different levels of the business. Examples of the different ways policy deployment is implemented include Hoshin planning and management by objectives. In order to implement policy deployment successfully, the organization should:

- Use the action plans defined in the strategic plan to set sophisticated goals, targets, schedules, and owners.

- Use the cascaded high-level goals to establish departmental and functional goals, targets, schedules, and owners.

- Incorporate local goals in order to define the performance plans for teams and individuals.

- Perform regular reviews to gauge the performance and achievement of the high-level as well as local goals.

- Link the performance of management to established goals when setting up the bonus structure.

Step Four: Recognize the Core Business Processes

All businesses are engaged in processes that are designed to transform some type of input into outputs that customers are willing to pay for. It is important for the organization to define clearly what these processes are, how they satisfy customers, and then document them. In order to understand how to examine the performance of processes and consequently identify the areas that need improving, the following terms should be applied:

- Level 1 processes – These are central business processes that are linked to a business function and can be traced through accounting records.

- Level 2 processes – These are sub-processes of level 1 and comprise a series of process steps that are distinctly related.

- Work steps – This is a work unit that falls under a level 2 process and comprises a series of tasks performed by either a small team or an individual.

The most effective way to determine which opportunities need to be improved is to first recognize which processes in the organization fall under level 1. These processes then have to be broken down so that the critical level 2 processes can be seen. Once this has been accomplished, Lean Six Sigma is then implemented in order to fix any problems in the work steps of the level 2 processes.

How to Identify, Prioritize, and Select Projects

There is a structured methodology that Black Belts, Master Black Belts, and Champions should follow to identify, prioritize, and choose Lean Six Sigma projects. In the initial phases of identifying and selecting a project, the Champion is supposed to help a trained Master Black Belt undertake the steps described below:

- Reviewing the strategic plan.

- Understanding the organization's high-level goals and objectives.

- Conducting a comparison between desired performance and actual performance for the entire organization.

- Understanding the departmental goals and objectives for every business function.

- Conducting a comparison between desired performance and actual performance for every individual business function.

- Identifying the core level 1 processes according to the analysis of goals, returns, and risks.

- Understanding the core level 2 processes according to the analysis of goals, returns, and risks.

- Brainstorming every potential improvement opportunity.

- Ranking and prioritizing every potential improvement opportunity according to goals, returns, and risks.

- Communicating the outcome of the ranking process to the team and establishing consensus.

- Launching Lean Six Sigma projects according to the prioritization schedule established previously.

Once this process is complete and well understood, the Champion is responsible for leading these steps regularly.

The Fundamental Role of the Champion

A Lean Six Sigma Champion performs various and diverse roles. These roles are dependent on how large the organization is and the scope of the deployment plan. Though the DMAIC methodology is a proven and effective way to solve problems and optimize performance, it still carries some risk of failure. If a Lean Six Sigma project is to achieve success, the Champion must be able to handle project risks and resolve organizational challenges, such as:

- Funding

- Scheduling

- Staffing

- Size and difficulty of the project

- Customer relations

- External elements

- General structure

- Project dependencies

The majority of the risks that crop up in a project can be addressed by ensuring that project identification is performed well, organizational priorities communicated clearly, and consensus built among the critical stakeholders.

The responsibilities of a Champion do not cease with the selection of the projects. The Champion must ensure that every project works according to a strong plan, has the resources required, and is effectively managed. The Champion must conduct effective performance reviews at the end of every DMAIC phase. These reviews are not to be restricted to the activities that have been completed, but should also explore how to successfully execute future phases.

Before and during project reviews, the Champion should be assisted by a well-trained Master Black Belt. There should also be a Black Belt who is trained in the use of technical tools. The Champion is ultimately responsible for ensuring adequate resources and eliminating obstacles to project success.

How to Select a Viable DMAIC Project

One of the most important components of project success is selecting the right project. In cases where practitioners are lax about selecting the right improvement opportunities, the end results are usually disastrous. It is not enough to simply choose a project based on a few obvious inputs or ease of completion. This "low-hanging fruit" approach may work in certain instances, but it should not define the approach that an organization uses, especially when priorities are not clear.

There must be a strong and consistent approach that helps determine whether a project will make a good DMAIC project, while also prioritizing projects according to resources allocated. To achieve this, certain selection criteria must be used.

Critical project criteria:
1. Customer impact – It must be determined whether project success will make a big difference in the way both internal and external customers perceive quality. This can be addressed through the use of a VOC analysis.

2. Service quality impact – It must be determined if service quality will be enhanced along the value chain. Though customers may be satisfied, it would be useless if the process ended up unwieldy and more complex.

3. Defect definition – The process defect must be defined well so that the project does not lose focus and become affected by scope creep. The final output should not be used as a measure of defect. For instance, failure to achieve revenue targets may be considered a high-level problem, but it should not be used as a defect metric. The defect metric must be an operational aspect, for example, cycle time, lead times, or rework rates.

4. Process stability – Before a process is improved, it must be checked for stability in performance. Stability does not have to mean desired performance has been attained. An unstable process may generate "noise" that may interfere with the accurate assessment of just how impactful the improvements will be.

5. Availability of data - There must be some data available in order to study a process and whether it needs to be improved. If the data is not available, it must at least be attainable. It is important to ensure that key data can be collected without needing to use up an unnecessary amount of resources.

6. Availability of a dedicated team – The organization requires dedicated Green and Black Belts to sustain the momentum of the project. Remember that the team members may have other daily functions to perform, so the time they spend on the project should be taken into account.

7. Benefits – Potential projects must be analyzed to determine their value. This is possible by using a discounted cash flow model. It is also necessary to include soft benefits like customer satisfaction and its impact on sales and retention.

8. Clarity of the solution – If the solution is already clear, there is no need to waste time with the DMAIC process. On the other hand, there may be many good solutions floated around, and it may be a good idea to look for the root causes instead of rushing to fix mere symptoms.

9. Project sponsorship – It cannot be stressed enough just how critical high-level project sponsorship is to Lean Six Sigma projects. Without it, project success will hang in the balance.

10. Project timeline – One of the best benchmarks to use when determining how reasonably fast a Lean Six Sigma project can be completed is the six-month mark. The viability of a DMAIC project is judged on whether it can be successfully completed within this time frame. If not, its feasibility diminishes.

11. Project alignment – The project must align with organizational strategic goals. If it does not, top management will be very reluctant to authorize it, much less finance it.

12. Probability of implementation – What are the chances of the solution being implemented in the organization? The resistance levels, rival initiatives, adjustment of strategic goals, and organizational changes are all factors that

should be assessed so as to determine the probability of implementation.

13. Control over inputs – Once some data has been collected, the team should evaluate if there will be enough inputs that can be measured and controlled. If it is not possible to exert reasonable control over the process inputs, it will be very difficult to achieve the project objectives.

14. Investment – How much money is it going to cost to fix the problem? If the project involves a large capital investment that may be difficult to regain, it does not satisfy the requirements of a good Lean Six Sigma improvement project.

It is extremely important that the right projects be identified and selected, and the right people are tasked with deployment. If an organization uses the right criteria throughout, there will be a higher chance for project success.

Part IV: Process Improvement

Chapter 10: The DMAIC Process and Tools

Lean Six Sigma uses DMAIC as a roadmap to provide a structured way to resolve business and process problems. The tools and methods used in DMAIC are extremely useful in determining, analyzing, and improving problems. However, most practitioners often apply these tools indiscriminately, not realizing that every tool is linked to a specific phase of DMAIC, and should, therefore, be used separately and sequentially.

That is why it is important to always refer to the concept of $Y = f(x)$ whenever the DMAIC process is being used. This mathematical equation is translated to "Y is a function of x." In other words, the output of the business process (Y) results from the inputs (x's) within the process. DMAIC seeks to identify those few variables and process inputs that are primarily responsible for influencing the process output. Every DMAIC phase should, therefore, be considered on the basis of how it helps achieve this goal.

Define Phase

This phase involves understanding the project Y and ways of measuring it. The team is tasked with defining the project goals and customer deliverables.

Steps in the Define phase:

- Defining the customers, their requirements, and their expectations (CTQs)

- Developing the problem statement, problem goals, and benefits

- Identifying the change champion and process team

- Defining the resources to be used

- Assessing crucial organizational support

- Developing the project plan and its milestones

- Developing a high-level process map

Tools used:

1. Project charter

This is a document that is designed to establish a structure and objective for the process improvement project. It incorporates seven elements:

Business Case – It enables the project team to understand how to link the project to the organization's overall goals. Business case clarifies the rationale behind undertaking the project and how it will advance organizational goals.

Problem Statement – It is a statement that describes in quantitative terms the problem with the current process. Questions that need to be asked include: What is the problem? Where does it hurt? What is its magnitude? What are its consequences? The problem statement is not supposed to point fingers or offer a solution.

Goal Statement – It provides a clear definition of the improvement the project team wants to accomplish. The goal statement must always begin with a verb, and should not assume to know the cause or solution. It must be SMART (Specific, Measurable, Attainable, Relevant, and Time-bound).

Project Scope – It provides insight into what the project deliverables will cover. It helps the team understand where the project will start and end, as well as project dimensions and constraints. Without a proper scope, the team will lose their motivation because the project will be too broad and difficult to implement. Longitudinal scoping involves fixing the start and end points of the project, while latitudinal scoping involves establishing the breadth of the project.

Project Milestone – It specifies the time allocated for completing each project phase. It involves a project plan (Gantt chart) and a communication plan, which should be linked to the DMAIC phases.

Resources and Team Roles – There must be enough

resources allocated to the project to successfully implement it. The top management, Deployment Leader, and Lean Six Sigma Champion are responsible for making sure that the project team is trained and equipped accordingly.

2. Process maps

A process map is a tool that is used to graphically depict the steps, inputs, outputs, and other relevant details pertaining to a process. It helps to illustrate the practical relationships between the different elements of a process. There are two types of process maps:

Process Flowchart – It is a simple logical sequence of activities within a process.

Deployment Flowchart - It is also referred to as a Swimlane flowchart and is used to describe the various roles of each stakeholder or department involved in a process.

3. SIPOC diagram

This is a diagram that illustrates the cross-functional activities undertaken within a process. It enables the team to identify suppliers, process inputs (x), process owner, outputs (Y), and customers. It also helps to identify and create limits for the process. It incorporates five elements:

Supplier – The entity providing inputs for the process.

Input – The data or product used within a process to deliver output.

Process – The activities undertaken in order to deliver output and satisfy customer needs.

Output – The results of a successful process.

Customer – The entity receiving the outputs.

4. Voice of Customer gathering
This is the statement the customer makes regarding a specific product or service. This has been extensively covered in Chapter 5, so there is no need to go through it again.

5. Critical-To-Quality drilldown tree
A CTQ drilldown tree is an effective tool used for converting the needs and requirements of customers into measurable characteristics. It is what creates a link between the project and the business, and helps manage the project.

Measure Phase

This phase involves prioritizing potential x's and measuring x's and Y. It is measuring the process to find out current performance.

Steps in the Measure phase:
- Defining the defects, opportunities, units and metrics from multiple sources

- Developing a data collection plan

- Collecting data

- Validating the measurement system

- Developing the $Y = f(x)$ relationship

- Determining Sigma baseline and process capability

Tools used:

1. Sampling

This is a data collection strategy that involves picking a select number of elements out of a larger target group. All the elements that are of interest to the study constitute the population. The group of elements that are actually studied is the sample. For example, the population would be all the employees in an organization, and the sample would be a small group of randomly chosen employees. Sampling methods include:

Simple random sampling – Every element has an equal chance of being chosen.

Stratified random sampling – Groups are formed depending on certain characteristics, and then elements are chosen randomly from each group.

Systematic sampling – Every n^{th} element is chosen from the population.

Cluster sampling – Clusters of elements are chosen after a specific interval.

Convenience sampling – It is dependent on access and convenience.

Judgment sampling – It is dependent on the belief that the elements chosen fit the requirements.

Quota sampling – It focuses on the representation of

particular features.

Snowball sampling – It depends on references made by others with similar characteristics.

2. Measurement system analysis

This is a technique used to understand the variations that can possibly arise due to the measurement system being used. The aim is to determine the most suitable tool for analysis depending on the type of data. For continuous data, Gage Repeatability and Reproducibility (R&R) is used, while for discrete data, Discrete Data Analysis (DDA) is used.

Two types of variation cause variations in a process. Actual Process Variation is the result of controllable factors or uncontrollable factors. Variation from Measurement System is the result of errors made by the operator or a flaw in the measurement instrument used.

3. Process sigma calculation

Process Sigma is a measurement gauge used to assess the output of a process and compare it to the performance standard. The higher the process sigma is, the higher the capability of the process. Process sigma enables the project team to have a common platform for comparing processes that may normally be measured using different tools.

Analyze Phase

This phase involves analyzing and determining the root causes of defects and opportunities for improvement. The aim is to quantify the x-Y relationship.

Steps in the Analyze phase:
- Defining performance objectives

- Identifying value-added and non-value added process steps

- Prioritizing opportunities to improve

- Determining root causes

- Identifying sources of variation

- Determining what the x's are

Tools Used:

1. Process Map analysis

A process map is a graphical illustration of every activity in a process that is performed in order to deliver an output. It helps to understand the inputs that are used to generate outputs. It helps explain which inputs are controllable and which ones are not. It defines the activities that are value-added and those that are non-value-added. Process map analysis also helps provide information regarding the location of bottlenecks in the process.

2. Why Analysis

This tool involves asking a series of "Why?" questions in order to determine the possible solutions to process variations and defects. For example, a lending institution may be interested to find out why its loan application process requires more than 14 working days for a customer to be declared credit worthy. The Why Analysis would be as follows:

- Why does the loan approval process take longer than 14 days? Most application forms are returned with blank fields.

- Why are the fields blank? Customers failed to fill in the required details.

- Why did the customer not fill in the required details? They didn't understand the information that was required.

- Why couldn't the customer understand the requirements on the form? The directions on the form are not clear.

- Why aren't the directions on the application form not clear? The print is too small to read.

3. Hypothesis testing

This is a tool that can be used to detect whether there are statistical differences between data sets. The aim is to determine if the data represents diverse distributions. The steps include:

- Determining an appropriate hypothesis test

- Stating the null and alternate hypotheses

- Calculating test statistics

- Interpreting the results – accepting or rejecting the null hypothesis

Improve Phase

This phase involves improving the process by developing creative solutions to eliminate defects.

Steps in the Improve phase:

- Performing experiments

- Creating innovative solutions

- Defining operating tolerances of the potential system

- Assessing failure modes of potential solutions

- Selecting and implementing the best solution

- Re-evaluating potential solution

Tools Used:

1. Failure Mode Effect Analysis (FMEA)
FMEA is a tool used to identify any potential failure modes that may occur in a process or product. The aim is to prioritize these failure modes using a score based on Severity (S), Occurrence (O), and Detectability (D). The scores range from 1 to 10, where 1 is the lowest and 10 the highest.

Risk Priority Number (RPN) = S*O*D

The equation above is then used to develop contingency plans to mitigate the risks. Severity defines the degree to which the failure will impact the Critical Quality Parameter. Occurrence refers to how frequently a variation arises. Detectability refers to the ability of the current control measures to detect a variation before failure mode occurs.

2. Pilot Solution Implementation

This is a technique used to test the effectiveness of a potential solution prior to implementing it in a process. It can be used to test a portion or the entire solution. Piloting is always a good idea in cases where the scope of variability is large, which may result in unforeseen consequences. Once a solution has been implemented and the process has changed, reversing the solution can be difficult. Piloting helps to avoid situations such as this. The steps involved include:

- Top management leadership and control

- Choosing a pilot team

- Holding meetings with the pilot team

- Planning strategies for effective execution

- Selling the new ideas to affected employees

- Training relevant employees for execution of pilot program

- Implementation of pilot program on shop floor

- Debriefing and expansion of pilot program if initially successful

3. Brainstorming: Opportunity Matrix

Before process improvement is conducted within an organization, there must be effective brainstorming to generate ideas on it will be done. The steps include:

- Gathering experts from diverse departments

- Identifying a long list (25-150) of potential root causes of a problem. The aim is to come up with as many root causes as possible, and may take a couple of hours. No judging of others ideas.

- Interviewing contributors who were not included in the brainstorming session, for example, former or present operations personnel. Additional root causes are collected.

- An Excel worksheet is generated showing every root cause, its ID number, initials of the proposer, and any further comments. The file is sent to all team members who are then asked to rank the root causes in order of importance - 1 represents "not important at all" while 10 is "extremely important." They are also asked to rate the estimated cost of every root cause, as well as indicate who should be considered a Champion for attacking a specific cause.

- The team leader receives the files back for collation. The cost, importance, Champion, and proposer rankings are calculated. The standard deviation of the importance rating is also calculated.

- An opportunity matrix is created, showing the importance ratings on the y-axis and the cost rating on the x-axis. The root causes are depicted as bubbles within the matrix and are indicated using their individual ID numbers. The size of the bubble represents the standard deviation of the importance ranking. The smaller the bubble, the greater the consensus. The root causes to be looked into further are picked according to their level of importance and consensus.

Control Phase

This phase involves monitoring the Y and important x's over time. The aim is to control the new improvements as well as the future performance of the process.

Steps in the Control phase:

- Defining and validating the monitoring and control system

- Developing standards

- Implementing statistical process control

- Determining process capability

- Developing the handoff plan to the process owner

- Verifying benefits, cost savings, and growth of profits

- Finalizing project documentation
- Celebrating

Tools Used:

1. Control Charts

A control chart can be used as a tool to observe the control and stability of a process. It can also serve as an analysis tool. Control charts are ideal for identifying variations in a process. A stable and controlled process tends to display some variation, though this variation is inherent to that process. In other words, it is possible to predict how the process will vary, within certain limits, in future. An unstable process, on the other hand, tends to display special or non-random variation caused by external factors.

Processes are generally classified as either ideal, threshold, brink of chaos, or state of chaos. An ideal state is where the process is predictable, stable, and in 100% conformance to expectations. Threshold state is where the process is predictable, still stable, but does not conform to customer needs as consistently as it should. Brink of chaos state is where the process is unpredictable, unstable, but still meets customer needs some of the time. It is only a matter of time before defects start to occur. State of chaos is where the process is unpredictable, uncontrollable, and does not conform to requirements at all.

In an organization, all processes are in constant flux between these states and are always shifting towards state of chaos. Most companies only take improvement measures when they experience a state of chaos. By using a control chart, it would be possible to detect such natural shifts toward degradation and improve the process much earlier.

The elements of a control chart include:

- A time series graph.

- The process location – This is a line drawn horizontally through the center of the data points, and is used to detect changes in trends.

- Upper and lower control limits – These are calculated using available data and are drawn equidistant from the center line.

It is clear that there are very many useful tools that can be used under the DMAIC methodology. It is up to practitioners to understand which tools to use for a particular phase in order to achieve the best results.

Chapter 11: Value Addition and Waste

In business, a value-added process can be described as a series of activities that meet the following three criteria:

1. The activities must in some way change the product or service.

2. The customer must be willing to pay for the output of the process.

3. The process activities must be performed the right way the first time round.

The Seven Types of Waste

Waste is a by-product that can be produced by almost every business activity within an organization. Waste exists in many different forms – some are obvious while others are hidden. This can make identification of waste a problem. In Lean Six Sigma, waste can be categorized into seven groups:

1. Defects - This type of waste includes products or services that do not conform to the standards of quality that the customer expects. It also includes any raw materials that a product manufacturer rejects due to their poor quality. Such factors translate into longer production times and increased dissatisfaction among customers, both internal and external.

2. Overproduction – This is the type of waste that occurs when production processes are allowed to continue despite there being no need to do so. Once the production targets have been met and goals accomplished, the process is allowed to continue, leading to the manufacturing of excess products. This form of waste also includes production of goods before they are required, not to mention the excess transport costs incurred.

3. Unnecessary Transportation – This is where there is excess transportation of products in the form of unnecessary movements within the facility. It is a result of poor design of the production facility, where processing is done by a number of different departments rather than within one cell environment. This type of waste also includes damage to products during transportation, as well as unnecessarily long transport times.

4. Waiting – This is waste that results from an assembly line or subassembly process that is not moving. In other words, it is a period of inactivity where a machine or worker has stopped working. For example, an employee leaves their workstation to get more raw materials yet there is another employee waiting to receive a product

part from the first employee. The time wasted does not add profitability to the process and costs the organization money.

5. Inventory – This is waste in the form of excess inventory. Capital is needlessly tied up in raw, work-in-process, as well as finished products. The inventory does not add value to the current production order in any way. The main cause of this type of waste is a lack of storage space. The organization should only produce what it is able to sell according to current customer demand, or else it will end up with excess products that no one wants. This can also lead to obsolescence and damage to products.

6. Motion – This is waste from excess motion, probably due to employee ergonomics that are not ideal. Employees, machines, and raw materials waste time moving pointlessly from place to place.

7. Over-processing - This includes those extra processes that a product undergoes due to inefficiencies. The entire process uses up more time and tools than actually needed for the desired result. Over-processing can be a result of defects, poor storage or handling. This forces employees to spend time performing extra inspections rather than producing new products.

Applying the Seven Wastes to Transactional Processes

The seven wastes can be used in manufacturing as well as transactional processes. However, when it comes to transactional processes, they can be applied in a simpler and logical manner. For example, assume that there are two departments involved in a transactional process, with an activity conducted by Department A ending up being reworked by Department B. A team is tasked with improving the process to eliminate waste. The team examines the current process and comes up with these questions:

- Are all process activities performed correctly, consistently, and in a sequential manner? Does each activity add value?

- Have the interfaces within and between departments been defined? Are they working? Is it clear who owns a particular interface?

- Are the decision-making criteria clear and well understood?

- Are there any dangling process steps? Some steps could lead nowhere, either because there is no clear customer or process output.

- Does the process include rework to fix defects? Where do the defects originate?

These key questions can help practitioners improve the process. In order to illustrate how these questions can be used to eliminate the seven wastes and improve a process, the following eight problem scenarios and their improvement actions are presented.

Problem 1: Activity performed inaccurately or inconsistently.

According to the payment process of a company, customers

were supposed to match payments to the right accounts before the next billing cycle. However, this was not possible 10% of the time, forcing the funds to go into a suspense account. The company had to get 16 people to work on nothing else but investigating these suspended payments.

The process was mapped and a total of ten different ways to resolve the issue were discovered. The solutions were explored and most found to be inefficient. The improvement team picked the best solution and all the employees were trained on the new method. The company was able to cut the staff investigating the suspended payments by half.

Improvement actions: Guidance and work instructions were provided. Trained personnel were held accountable.

Problem 2: Activity not performed in right sequence.

Employees in most organizations today are required to show their ID badges when entering a building. In some cases, they have to use their badges to access the company's computers. Though similar information is scanned for the two processes, they are usually viewed as distinct processes. The outcome is that the company loses productivity through new recruits or individuals transferred to different departments.

The company decides to combine these two ID requirements and instructs new employees accordingly. Before they start work, HR ensures their security information is uploaded. When new employees arrive for work, they are immediately dispatched to IT and security departments to begin the ID badge process. Then they are directed to sign up with payroll. Finally, they receive their badges.

Improvement action: The sequence of activities was changed.

Problem 3: Too much cycle time for loan application process.

A financial institution discovers that it takes 21days for a loan application to be approved. A loan application form is usually sent to different departments for approval. An improvement team tracked one document and found out that it traveled all over the building. They measured the linear distance the document traveled and discovered that it moved a whopping 5,000 feet! It was decided to locate all the relevant departments around one area of the building. This led to a 4,800-foot reduction in distance traveled. The loan approval period was also cut to 3 days.

Improvement action: Elimination of the biggest non-value-added steps.

Problem 4: Inoperable interface

A team was tasked with improving the document-scanning process, with the goal being to minimize overall costs. The team found out that one of the document feeders of the scanning machines stored all the relevant information in electric form, but the organization still required the documents to be printed and sent to the scanning department. This led to a huge surge in workload for the scanning department, and also cost the company a lot of money in terms of paper. Its carbon footprint also increased. This indicated a failure by the company to map the whole process from start to finish.

Improvement actions: Clear definition of the interface and assigning accountability and ownership.

Problem 5: Improper decision-making processes

Sometimes organizations fail to clearly define the decision criteria that should be used in a transactional process. This can easily lead to variation in the way employees interpret policies. An improvement team conducted a review of a mortgage company's audit process. It was discovered that different auditors used different criteria to approve mortgages, and furthermore, the underwriters were also using diverse criteria. The result was that some people whose loans should have been declined received approval, and some who should have been approved were declined. It also led to time being wasted reconciling audit results.

The team reviewed the company's risk models and credit policies in order to clearly define terms. All the underwriters were also trained and random analysis checks conducted to ensure consistency in decision-making.

Improvement actions: Clarification of operational definitions, training of employees, and reviewing decisions.

Problem 6: Redundant Processes

These are processes that may have been of value long ago but are no longer required. They have been in place for so long that nobody has noticed that they are adding no value in a process. This is why it's important for Lean Six Sigma Belts to challenge the status quo and eliminate processes that lead nowhere. A good example is the fact that most organizations have in place a system where expense reports must be approved by several departments. This causes unnecessary delays and breeds mistrust.

Improvement action: Eliminate redundant steps

Problem 7: Rework Loop

There are numerous cases of rework in transactional processes. One department prepares official documents and sends them to another department. The receiving department discovers that some of the documents have not been filled in properly. This forces employees there to stop their own work to fix the problems. This can easily become an institutional problem. The rework loop can only be eliminated by changing the organizational culture. Employees must be trained to take responsibility for the quality of their work rather than always expecting other people to check it for them.

Improvement action: Identify the root causes of rework, eliminate them, and track the changes.

Chapter 12: The Process Improvement Team

Improving the processes within an organization is not an easy task for most managers. There are numerous responsibilities to take care of and fires to put out. The resources to implement the improvement is lacking in most cases. Indeed, there are numerous obstacles that prevent organizations from effectively deploying Lean Six Sigma. However, one way to leverage available resources and apply the methodology is to assemble a cross-function improvement team.

A process improvement team is a group of people within an organization handpicked to improve a process. The team is made up of employees who are either directly or indirectly involved in the process. The responsibility for picking and managing the team lies with the process owner and team leader, though it has to be sponsored by a senior manager. The team uses Lean Six Sigma tools to achieve their objectives.

On the other hand, some organizations choose to apply a

management-led initiative, where managers start the process improvement themselves. They meet and discuss issues regarding process improvement and cost reduction. Once they come up with ideas, management communicates the improvements that need to be implemented all over the organization. The recommendations trickle downwards, with supervisors policing the initiative and workers executing the orders.

Disadvantages of a Management-Led Process

Compared to a team-led improvement process, this strategy has many innate weaknesses.

- The managers who are brainstorming for solutions are not in direct contact with the process in question, which means that they are likely to address perceived rather than actual issues.

- Since responsibility for success is placed on management and supervisors, they will have to deal with a bigger workload.

- Frontline management and the workforce are ignored and feel no sense of ownership of the initiative. This may lead to a lack of enthusiasm to see the project succeed.

- Information moves from senior management downwards, thus creating room for confusion and miscommunication.

Benefits of Team –Led Process

- The people who generate ideas and solutions for improvements are those who know the process inside out. They want to see these issues resolved.

- Ideas move from the bottom upwards. This makes the frontline staff feel as if they own the process and enthusiastic for the initiative.

- It emphasizes teamwork and makes the workforce feel appreciated.

- The team is able to quickly recognize solutions that are easily implementable, thus saving the organization money and improving the process immediately.

How to Create a Good Team

For a team to be successful in its endeavors, it is important to have a good structure and composition.

- The team should comprise people who know the process well and are diverse in their thinking. There should be some process experts as well as suppliers and customers.

- A team leader should be appointed. They should have a firm understanding of the process and experience in project management. They must also be knowledgeable in the application of Lean Six Sigma and its tools. This position can be given to a trained Green Belt.

- The team should be manageable in size. Ideally, there should be not more than eight members so as to ensure full participation by all.

- Meeting times should be established in a way that allows everyone to attend.

- The first meeting should be about the establishment of ground rules. All members need to be informed about what is expected in terms of attendance and participation.

- A team recorder should be appointed. Their job is to record any good ideas that members come up with.

Guidelines for Selecting Lean Six Sigma Candidates

If a Lean Six Sigma project is to provide the intended benefits, the right candidates need to be selected. This means that Green Belts and Black Belts who possess the required traits must be identified before the program kicks off. The guidelines described here can also be helpful when choosing which Green Belts are ready to transition into Black Belt status.

Traits for Green Belt Candidates

These candidates must have shown proficiency in starting and finishing projects while solving problems using a data-based approach. Their traits include:

1. Interest in Lean Six Sigma – It is critical to have an interest in improving existing processes. This is shown by participation in improvement programs and a proven track record of doing quality work.
2. Process orientation – A Green Belt needs to visualize the entire process and how the various components interact to produce the required output.
3. Knowledge of the process – It is very important to understand how the project will impact the organization as a whole.
4. Passion – The candidate needs to show excitement and dedication in being part of the initiative.
5. Enthusiasm to learn – A Green Belt usually learns about many tools and techniques. These need to be practiced, not just during training hours but even beyond. This will only be possible if the individual has the zeal to learn.

Traits for Black Belt Candidates
This role places more emphasis on leadership qualities, which makes it a bit different from that of a Green Belt. Middle managers can make good Black Belts. A Black Belt is required to possess the same traits as a Green Belt as well as satisfy the criteria described below:

1. Possess technical skills – This is a critical factor, as a candidate needs to be able to apply high-level technical skills during a Lean Six Sigma project.

2. Have business acumen – As a leader, a Black Belt must be knowledgeable about the current market the organization exists in, identify the daily challenges the business faces, and thus push the program in the right direction.

3. Be an influential personality – When leading teams, the Black Belt will need to give direction to people, communicate well with the different management levels, and help the organization implement change.

4. Possess problem-solving skills – A Black Belt must have proven their data analysis skills in past projects.

5. Have a mentorship attitude – A Black Belt is responsible for training and mentoring Green Belts. They are required to provide expertise and help eliminate any potential obstacles. In some cases, they will have to conduct training for Lean Six Sigma awareness.

Project Definition and Identification of Root Causes

Once the team has been created, the team must establish a charter and define the project. This is a document that explains and quantifies the problem that needs to be solved, the team's goals, and time allocated for every step in the project. At this time, the team leader needs to identify every member's strengths and interests and assign responsibilities accordingly. It is much easier for people to execute tasks if those tasks are aligned with their strengths and interests.

The metric that represents the performance of the process should be identified. For example, if the team has identified throughput as a problem, then the metric could be defects. A Pareto chart is an appropriate analysis tool for this as it illustrates defects by type as well as the total number of defects. The team also needs to make sure that the metric used is an actual indicator of process performance. Assumptions should not be made as this will lead to wastage of time. A control chart can also be used to monitor the metric and provide control limits.

Once the team has completed the process of identifying the metric, it is time to brainstorm for improvement ideas. The Pareto chart can be used to unearth root causes of problems and also generate solutions. Other tools that can be used during the brainstorming session include a cause-and-effect diagram. Every team member needs to be encouraged to take part. Every idea should be recorded and ultimately rated according to impact. In case there are any ideas that can clearly be implemented quickly, the team should inform the project sponsor so that quick action can be taken.

Planning, Monitoring, and Control

The team needs to allocate resources to the tasks that will lead to improvement of the process. Timelines must also be set for every task. The team can use a Gantt chart or a spreadsheet to monitor tasks, members responsible, target dates, and status of tasks. The Gantt chart is a good way to develop an agenda for future meetings. Task progress must be tracked weekly and any roadblocks eliminated.

One of the simplest ways to track the impact that an action is having is by correlating the start date of every task with the performance of the process. The control chart is useful for this purpose. Activities that are implemented to minimize defects will display themselves on the control chart as process shifts. As the tasks are implemented one by one, the control chart should be indicating that the process is moving closer to what the team established at the beginning.

It is important that the team develops a transition plan once the goals of the project have been achieved. There needs to be a system in place where the critical process tasks can still be maintained without ongoing support from the improvement team. This should be the responsibility of the process owner.

The Role of the Process Owner

In a company that has experience implementing Lean Six Sigma projects, it is easy to hear stories of how the Black Belt led a project improvement team that saved the business millions of dollars. There will be stories swirling everywhere about how the Master Black Belt solved a technical problem that the company had been struggling with for years. Even the Champion will get a lot of credit for the amazing results that have been seen.

Yes, it is true that these people deserve credit for how they used their Six Sigma credentials to help the company. However, there is one group of people who do an excellent job but are never recognized enough. They are the ones who are truly responsible for maintaining the gains of Lean Six Sigma long after the Belts have left the scene. These are the process owners.

The process owner is an individual who is tasked with determining how a process runs and bears responsibility for ensuring that it continues to satisfy customer and business needs now and for years to come. Every organization that wants to keep the Lean Six Sigma momentum going needs to recognize the role of the process owner.

Responsibilities of the Process Owner

1. They understand the critical aspects of the process. The process owner knows the elements of the output that the customers and the business value the most. They also need to deeply understand how their process aligns with the goals of the company.

2. They track the performance of the process using data. The data used needs to be input metrics as well as output measures. Input metrics are useful because they help to predict performance from an early stage. In most instances, the process owner tracks data that is already compiled by other process operators.

3. They ensure that the process is well documented, and the documentation is standardized and updated often. An organization must always strive to reduce variations in the way employees operate a process. The process owner is responsible for identifying best practices and standardizing the process in order to guarantee output quality. The best practices must be documented in form of flow charts or other visual methods and updated regularly.

4. They establish a process management plan that everyone working with the process can see. This plan also contains response plan in case signs of trouble are detected.

5. They hold reviews on a regular basis. These include a process review, where questions are asked regarding customer satisfaction, control of input/output metrics, and persons assigned to deal with any process problems. Another type of review is the process management

review, where questions are asked about how effective the process monitoring and managing methods are.

6. They ensure that all solutions that the improvement team identified are integrated and sustained in the process.

7. They ensure that the process operators are well trained and have enough resources to perform their duties effectively.

8. They provide the vital link between the process and customers. The process is the one person who must stay connected to everyone else, whether it is internally or externally.

The role the process owner plays may seem boring and routine, but nevertheless, it is extremely critical to the organization. They do not work alone, and the process operators that work under them also help to manage the process. However, at the end of the day, the process owner is who has the authority and responsibility to make decisions regarding the process.

Chapter 13: Design For Lean Six Sigma

When an organization says that it is using Lean Six Sigma, it is usually assumed that the methodology in play is DMAIC. This is true in most cases because many organizations have existing processes that are generating a lot of waste. However, there is an alternative approach that is used primarily by organizations that are looking to design a brand new product or process, and want to ensure that it meets quality standards. This approach is known as Design For Six Sigma (DFSS).

DFSS

This is an emergent approach whose main objective is to create a new product or service that is free from defects, while also implementing Lean Six Sigma early in its lifecycle. DFSS enables an organization to enhance the rate and quality of its design process.

The DFSS approach is quite different from the DMAIC methodology. The phases of DFSS are yet to be universally defined, with most companies or training organizations implementing their own variation. Most organizations will tailor DFSS to fit their business, industry, or cultural needs. If they are hiring the services of a consulting company, they will simply adopt the version of DFSS that the consultant recommends. This is why DFSS is considered to be more of an approach rather than a clearly defined methodology.

DFSS can be implemented when designing or redesigning a product or service from scratch. It is expected that a product or service designed via DFSS will have a process Sigma level of at least 4.5, which translates to not more than 1 defect in every 1000 opportunities. However, depending on the product, the Sigma level can sometimes be as high as 6 or more. It is clearly very difficult to design and launch a new product or service that has such a low level of defects. In order to achieve this, the organization must ensure that customer needs and expectations (CTQs) are fully understood prior to completion and implementation of a design.

DFSS Methodology

The first step in the DFSS methodology is identifying and analyzing gaps that may negatively affect the performance of a new process, product or service. The main focus is on how customers respond to the new item. Once this information has been obtained, it is then possible for the organization to establish a project to deal with the problems.

There are a number of variations of the DFSS approach. These include DMADV, DMADOV, DCCDI, IDOV, and DMEDI. They may differ slightly from one another but they essentially follow similar steps and aim to achieve similar objectives. DFSS approaches are a way of designing processes, products, and services to minimize development costs and delivery time, improve effectiveness, and enhance customer satisfaction.

The basic procedure is as described below:

- Capturing of customer requirements

- Analysis and prioritization of requirements

- Development of the design

- Tracking the capability of the process, product or service at every step

- Exposing gaps between customer requirements and product capabilities.

- Establishing a control plan.

Implementing DFSS

Most organizations that implement DFSS tend to focus too much on financial accountability at the expense of implementation accountability. It is important that organizations that choose to implement DFSS place emphasis on staying true to the DFSS process. This should be translated into the disciplined and thorough application of DFSS tools, for example, QFD (Quality Function Deployment), transfer functions, tolerance allocation, expected value analysis, and others. Refusing to apply DFSS tools in a design process will not produce the expected benefits.

When implementing DFSS, the organization must believe that the powerful tools that form part of DFSS will bring the intended benefits. However, there are signs that most companies are reluctant to implement DFSS yet they expect to reap savings directly. This fear of putting in the hard work that is part of DFSS leads organizations to take shortcuts that do more harm than good in the long run.

The business world is constantly buzzing with talk of the desire for culture change. If the powerful tools available are not being implemented, this culture change will happen very slowly, even with top management pushing the agenda. Achieving breakthrough improvement and change go hand in hand with using the tools available. When deploying DFSS, it is important to remember that using the tools will produce results, which means implementation accountability must be pushed to the fore. It bears just as much importance as financial accountability, and in fact, is much easier to monitor.

Benefits of Implementing DFSS

1. DFSS has been proven to provide a gain of one sigma quality level over previous designs.

2. DFSS reduces the time it takes to get a product or service into the market.

3. It can be easily applied to any type of organization, product, or service.

4. It is a very cost effective way to eliminate defects from a system. Costs of production are usually lowest during the initial phases of design, thus giving DFSS a high performance/cost ratio.

5. It offers a disciplined approach when it comes to accountability of implementation.

6. The DFSS scorecard enables enhanced and more consistent collection of data.

7. The DFSS data and scorecard help to highlight the potential causes of failure rather than depending on assumptions.

Differences between DFSS and DMAIC

1. DMAIC is used when improving a process that is already in place while DFSS is used when developing an entirely new process.

2. DFSS is considered a preventative approach rather than a curative one. Organizations implement DMAIC methodology only when they identify flaws in the process and try to eliminate waste. With DFSS, the defects are eliminated while the process is being designed.

3. DFSS is considered to be more economically viable than DMAIC since defects are eliminated during the initial stages of process/product/service design.

4. The tools used in the implementation of DFSS are quite different from those in the DMAIC methodology. In fact,

the reason why DFSS was created was because DMAIC tools could not be used to optimize a process beyond three or four Sigma without having to redesign the fundamentals. The best option was to design for quality from the start.

DMADV

This is a popular DFSS methodology that has five phases:

Define – Customer goals and project goals are defined.

Measure – Customer needs and requirements are determined. Industry benchmarks are also set.

Analyze – Options are analyzed to satisfy customer needs.

Design – Detailing how customer needs are to be met.

Verify – Verification of whether performance will be able to satisfy customers.

DMADOV

This is a slight modification of the DMADV methodology. It contains an *Optimize* phase where advanced statistical models and tools are used to optimize performance.

DCCDI

Define – Definition of project goals.

Customer - Completion of customer analysis.

Concept – Development, review, and selection of ideas.

Design - Detailing how customer needs and business specifications are to be met.

Implementation – Development and commercialization of the product or service.

IDOV

This methodology is well known in manufacturing circles.

Identify – Finding out the customer CTQs and specifications.

Design – Customer CTQs are translated into functional needs and further into potential solutions. The best solution is chosen from the list.

Optimize – Advanced statistical models and tools are used to optimize performance.

Validate – Ensuring that the design will satisfy customer CTQs.

DMEDI

Define – Identifying business problems and customer desires.

Measure – Customer needs and requirements are determined.

Explore – Analysis of the business process and exploring options for designs that will meet customer needs and specifications.

Develop – Delivering an ideal design as per customer needs.

Implement – Putting the new design through simulation tests to check efficacy to meet customer requirements.

It is evident that DFSS encompasses numerous methodologies. There are variations in the names as well as the number of phases. However, all the methods under DFSS utilize the same advanced techniques for design, for example, Failure Modes and Effects Analysis, Design of Experiments, Robust Design, Quality Function Deployment, etc.

Chapter 14: The Deployment Mistakes to Avoid

It is clear that deploying Lean Six Sigma produces great rewards for an organization. However, there are times when the whole deployment program fails, resulting in a lot of wasted time and resources. This is usually because of deployment mistakes that were not handled well. These mistakes need to be recognized and avoided at all costs. Here are the most common Lean Six Sigma deployment mistakes and how to resolve them:

Mistake #1: Weak Leadership Support

The major driver for the success of a Lean Six Sigma initiative is strong leadership commitment. The top management must support the initiative throughout the organization and ensure that there is action to back up their words. The solution is to keep the top leadership engaged in every stage of the process. Senior management must take the time to communicate with staff, stressing the need to focus on Lean Six Sigma as a way to achieve organizational objectives. The leadership must also allocate time for reviewing deployment progress during every management meeting.

Mistake #2: Too Broad a Scope

Whenever a Lean Six Sigma project fails, it is usually because of scope creep. If the scope is too broad from the beginning, there will not be enough focus to guarantee the improvement of a process, product or service. Sometimes the scope can even increase in the middle of the project. To avoid this problem, the team must concentrate on maintaining a narrow a scope as possible so that they do not bite off more than they can chew.

Mistake #3: Poor Deployment Strategy

The aim of having a deployment strategy is to ensure that organizational goals are aligned to deployment outcomes. If there is no alignment, the stakeholders will fail to see the point of the entire process. The solution to this problem is to make sure that the deployment results and business goals are aligned. The deployment strategy must take into account planning, employee training, project execution, information management, and achievement of operational excellence. There must be periodic review of the progress made on every strategy and its impact on business results. By monitoring these two elements, the team will be able to perform adjustments when necessary. When positive changes start to be seen, the organization begins to believe more in the effort.

Mistake #4: Too Much Emphasis on Training and Certification

It is easy to fall for the notion that everyone involved in a Lean Six Sigma project must know every detail about every complex statistical tool and technique. There are a lot of training and certification courses out there, with trainers and consultants competing heavily against each other to corner the market. As a result, there has been a lot of focus on teaching advanced tools and getting certified. The truth is that not every tool has to be used in every project. The solution is to place more emphasis on learning expediency and application of knowledge. An organization should remain focused on execution of the projects rather than how many certified Belts it has.

Mistake #5: Poor Project Selection

If the project improvement team loses focus from the beginning and does a shoddy job of selecting and prioritizing projects, disaster will strike. The project may be scrapped or delayed, thus causing cynicism among the Belts. The solution to this mistake is to make sure that data and goals are the key elements to focus on when selecting and prioritizing projects. There must be regular meetings to review data and customer, business and process goals. The team should also make sure that every project that is selected has a sponsor who will monitor and give approval for the project.

Mistake #6: Not Appointing a Deployment Leader

There are organizations that have tried to get away with

deploying Lean Six Sigma projects without designating a deployment leader. Without a deployment leader, the individual teams will engage in improvement activities in their own areas but there will be no real synergy or unity of purpose. This will lead to confusion and failure. The solution is to appoint a deployment leader whose responsibility is to train team members, assign projects, and select the tools to be used. A deployment leader is the one who provides direction and ensures general progress.

Mistake #7: Isolated Implementation

What point is there in improving a product's design but leaving the manufacturing process intact? Deploying small, localized improvement projects is not a smart strategy. It may be a good place to start if resources are minimal, but isolated and disconnected pockets of improvement will not realize the full benefits. With Lean Six Sigma, best organizational results are achieved when a pervasive implementation strategy is adopted. After all, organizations are made up of interconnected processes.

Conclusion

This book has gone a long way in explaining the most important aspects a beginner needs to know about Lean Six Sigma. The information presented here is a great place to begin your Lean Six Sigma journey.

The fundamental principles have been discussed, and the key elements that help achieve project success have been elaborated. Take the time to go through the chapters again in case there is some content that is unclear.

As always, there is no point in reading a book and not taking action. If you want to become a Lean Six Sigma Belt, put what has been learned into action. Keep learning and expanding your horizons by reading more advanced books.

We hope that you will use the information in this book as a steppingstone to further your knowledge and take your organization to the next level!

CPSIA information can be obtained
at www.ICGtesting.com
Printed in the USA
LVHW082244031221
705203LV00018B/2310

9 781541 059559